ANIMATION, THE BUSINESS
MECHANICAL AND ARCHITECTURAL VISUALIZATION

Bruce W. Jones

Prentice Hall

Upper Saddle River, New Jersey 07458

Library of Congress Cataloging-in-Publication Data

Jones, Bruce W.

Animation, the business : mechanical and architectural visualization / Bruce W. Jones.

p. cm.

ISBN 0-13-085112-4

1. Computer animation. I. Title.

TR897.7.J66 2000

006.6'96—dc21

00-025166

Publisher: Dave Garza
Acquisitions Editor: Elizabeth Sugg
Developmental Editor: Judy Casillo
Supervising Manager: Mary Carnis
Edictorial Assistant: Lara Dugan
Production Editor: Tally Morgan
Production Liaison: Denise Brown
Director of Manufacturing & Production: Bruce Johnson
Manufacturing Buyer: Ed O'Dougherty
Composition: Publishers' Design and Production Services, Inc.
Printer/Binder: Banta Harrisonburg
Cover Design: Lafortezza
Cover Art: Peter Maltz/Stock Illustration Source, Inc.
Creative Director: Marianne Frasco
Cover Design Coordinator: Miguel Ortiz

Prentice-Hall International (UK) Limited, *London*
Prentice-Hall of Austrailia Pty. Limited, *Sydney*
Prentice-Hall Canada Inc., *Toronto*
Prentice-Hall Hispanoamericana, S.A., *Mexico*
Prentice-Hall of India Private Limited, *New Delhi*
Prentice-Hall of Japan, Inc., *Tokyo*
Prentice-Hall Singapore Pte. Ltd.
Editora Prentice-Hall do Brasil, Ltda., *Rio de Janeiro*

TRADEMARK ACKNOWLEDGMENTS

3D Studio MAX 3.0 is a registered trademark of AutoDesk/Discreet.

AutoCAD is a registered trademark of AutoDesk.

Corel Draw, Zara, and Photo Paint are registered trademarks of Corel Systems Corporation.

Adobe Illustrator, Adobe PhotoShop, PostScript and the .EPS extension are registered trademarks of Adobe Systems, Incorporated.

ZIP and JAZ are registered trademarks of IOMEGA Corporation.

Fiery is a trademark of Electronics for Imaging, Inc.

HP Inkjet is a trademark of Hewlett Packard Corporation.

Plexiglass is a trademark of Plexiglass Plastics Corporation.

Rhino is a trademark of Robert McNeel & Associates.

Softimage is a trademark of Avid Technology Inc., Softimage Company.

ClothesReyes is a trademark of Infographica, Inc.

People for People is a registered trademark of People for People.

Indigo is a registered trademark of Silicon Graphics, Inc.

Poser is a registered trademark of Meta Creations.

Viewpoint and Viewpoint DataLabs are registered trademarks of Viewpoint DataLabs.

Credit is herein extended to the operators and artists who contributed to the www.3dcafe.com site and for the use of the people, trees, and cars from that site, used in the bank example.

A thank you is extended to The Peoples' Exchange Bank of Kentucky and Carlson Associates, Inc. for release of rights to print the bank image and AutoCAD drawings showcased in Job 3.

Trademarks of other products mentioned in this book are held by the companies producing them.

Show trademarks including but not limited to: SIGGRAPH, NAB, AutoDesk University, E3, Comdex, WindowsWorld, and IEEE are all trademarks held by their creators and sponsors.

10 9 8 7 6 5 4 3 2 1

ISBN 0-13-085112-4

Contents at a Glance

Job 1

The Flying Logo is now, and will for a long time be, the number one job done by students of animation after graduation. It is an opportunity to show what you can do in creativity and compositing. It has all the elements of 3D animation in their simplest form and should be seen as an opportunity for self-promotion.

Job 2

The mechanical device portion of the computer illustration and animation market has been growing slowly for many years now. Form, fit, and function studies of complex mechanisms and ergonomic use studies can all be enhanced through the use of computer graphics.

Job 3

The Architectural Fly-Around is a staple of small animation businesses. Architects have always valued visual aids for the presentation of their concepts to clients as well as a method to work out their ideas before construction. Pen, ink, markers, and watercolor have been the visualization media of choice for centuries. 3D models give the client an approximate view of the final product. Computer illustration and animation are tools that can show the client a picture of the finished facility without breaking ground.

CONTENTS

INTRODUCTION

My students, and occasionally clients, ask me "How long have you been into computer animation?" I give them the answer they want, "About nine years," and they are satisfied. The truth is that we are a product of all that we have done in our lives. Knowledge of any single piece of software will not get us too far. The engineering design and drafting work I have done with AutoCAD over the last 14 years, two years in a commercial art school in the late '60s, and growing up in a household where salesmanship talk and contract clauses and conditions were topics of dinner-table discussion are all part of my success as a computer animator.

In the series of which this book is a part, I will address both the technical how-to of each type of job using 3D Studio MAX and the broader picture of finding work, selling it, delivering it and the economics of doing it for profit.

It doesn't matter much whether you are opening a dairy farm, flipping burgers at Beef & Shake Heaven, or pitching real estate: you are involved in sales. Computer animation involves a sales pitch that requires technical expertise, corporate knowledge, artistic skill, and salesmanship of the first order. Because you aren't selling a familiar product, you must create your market. You must create a need for animation in the customer's mind, sell the price, interpret the customer's vision, and produce and deliver the product (and, hopefully, get more work from the customer in the future).

It is necessary to have some animation work to show potential clients before they are likely to offer you more animation work. My suggestion, though costly, is to work through as many of the exercises in the series as you can, outputting the results to videotape as you complete them. Produce still images and storyboards as you go along, and when you feel confident about the work you have produced, begin looking for contract work. Think of this as a self-directed education.

What you will need: a computer, software, plenty of creative talent and, later, a registered business name, a few business forms, and a customer.

ACKNOWLEDGMENTS

Thanks are due first to my wife, who did the final editing of this book, and four children who lost me during the year I completed this book and worked on my master's thesis.

Thanks are also due to my friends Kayanna Pace, for her electronic prepress editing; Sally Parsonson for her editing of my structure and grammar; Madeline Baum-Massara for content and technical editing; and Dean Ann Critchfield, who encouraged me to join the academic world and to stay there.

I also credit Billy Casanova, Robert Dessert, Kevin Christopher, Geoffrey Keene, and all those who took part in the Atlanta 3D Studio MAX users group during the past eight years, whose creative work and enthusiasm helped carry me, when animation was not the most popular kid on the block.

I extend my appreciation, too, to the instructors who reviewed this text in the course of its development: Scott F. Hall, SUNY Alfred State College; Robert King, ITT Technical Institute; Steve Missal, The Art Institute of Ft. Lauderdale; James Mohler, Purdue University; Scott Nelowet, The Art Institute of Ft. Lauderdale; and Pierre Pepin, The Art Institute of Ft. Lauderdale.

WHO SHOULD READ THIS BOOK?

This book is intended for the advanced beginner. It assumes that you have read the manuals that come with 3D Studio MAX and have done all the tutorials offered. The following material is intended to take you beyond the button-pushing sequences and tips and tricks for better looking files (there are many excellent books and tutorials on the Web that cover these areas), and offers insight into the business part of computer animation. This book focuses on efficient process rather than specific technique, a broad view of how the pieces fit together in the business rather than the math or language behind the program code.

JOB 1 THE FLYING LOGO

The flying logo is as much a part of the 3D modeling industry as the mouse is of cartooning. Every animator has started his career–often his first assignment–doing flying logo pieces. They can be as simple as a tracing from a business card that is then extruded into the third dimension and displayed against a blue sky with puffy white clouds, or elaborate explosions, burning planets, revolving flares, dramatic backlights, and endless environmental special effects. No matter how much glitter we place on, in, or around them, they are still flying logos and they are a requirement on your demo reel.

CHAPTER 1   GETTING THE JOB

OBJECTIVE

Take a few minutes and jot down the date, some notes about why you are reading this. Make some notes about where you think you are going and what you wish to accomplish.

It will be interesting for you to review these after you have completed the text and see if you have expanded your view of computer animation.

THE INITIAL MEETING

Work comes from everywhere and nowhere, in the middle of the night from someone that you forgot you met last year, to your Uncle Louie. Take it when it comes and do every job to the absolute best of your ability; little $500 jobs are often your ticket to larger projects.

Business meetings take place in donut shops, over pizza, in cars, on conference tables and over drawing boards in trailers. I have done sales pitches in $100 per meal restaurants and sitting on a pile of foam insulation in the middle of a factory floor.

The customer is always right. You learn very little by talking. Cultivate the lost art of not talking, but listening..

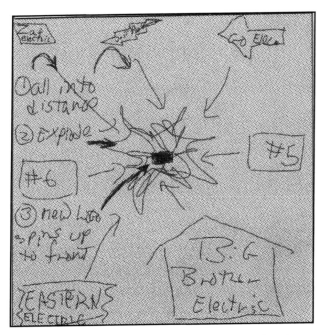

Cocktail napkins are the most available and, therefore, frequently used source of sketch paper for most luncheon or dinner meetings.

TAKING NOTES

Notes should be taken from the time a client calls through the job's progress. More notes should be made after the job is closed out. This clarifies details and documents the job's progress. Writing and reviewing these notes is the best way to review what you are doing right and where improvements can be made.

There are several excellent software packages for tracking leads and clients. For a small business, a stenographer's pad is an ideal tool for jottin down notes during the first conversation with a client. Be sure to date the pages at the beginning of each day and before picking up phone messages.

Once the dialog becomes serious enough for the lead to ask for a face-to-face meeting, that lead has become a potential client and deserves a file folder. A copy of the initial and subsequent conversations should be made and placed in the new file. Be certain that the notes are dated.

Copies of the bid, quote, contract (if any), faxed information, revisions to the proposals, unreturned material samples, disks with CAD files, a copy of the MAX file, copies of expense receipts, copies of the materials as scanned and any other correspondence with the client should immediately go into the file. The file should contain a notebook into which the job history is recorded as soon as a downpayment is received. Correspondence can be stapled into the pages of the notebook. Spiral-bound books prevent lost pages.

Notes are critically important. Rough or cryptic notes taken while meeting with the client must be translated quickly or their meaning will be lost. They should not be taken on a cocktail napkin, but if that is all that is available, it is better than not taking notes at all.

GETTING THE RIGHT DATE AND DATA

Put pencil and paper on your checklist of things to bring to every interview, no matter how casual. No one objects to your taking notes; everyone is annoyed when you forget an important detail and have to rewrite a proposal. Take notes on everything. Read the high points back to the client before you end the meeting. Create a commitment checklist of what is expected of you, and what the client is going to do as well, before the next meeting; prioritize these if possible. Set up a next meeting, or there will never be one. Be sure you have established that the work is being done for a fee, the latest possible delivery date, and the medium on which the final product is to be delivered.

Some examples of points you should determine before fees and deadline the following: Is the logo already in a vector format or is it raster or hard copy only? Do you have the exact Pantone or other color standard? Most corporations own a piece of music that they prefer to use on all company pieces; find out who has the master tape or file, and what rights they own to that music.

REVIEW YOUR NOTES IMMEDIATELY

As soon as you have waved good-bye to your client in the parking lot, sit in your car and review the notes on the meeting and prioritize what you must do to continue. Sometimes in the process of discussion you may forget that you agreed to check on some critical detail with your output resource that could limit the production. Now it is Friday at 4:00 and the client goes home to an unlisted number at 4:30 sharp.

Or maybe you agreed to fax the proposal before going to bed so your client could present it to his boss in the morning. If you are asked to fax overnight, get some coffee and get it out to their fax machine before you fall down for the night. The first request for something difficult is often created to test your ability to react quickly.

HAVE I GOT A DEAL FOR YOU!

When the client offers you a percentage rather than payment, pack it up and go home. Animation is not speculative work. You should be paid for your time, effort, and knowledge. It is a combination of art, consulting, science and acting; this is not the stock market. When a client offers a flat fee plus a percentage of the gross (not net) then you have to consider that the percentage may never happen and decide whether you can take that financial hit and gamble. Gambling is what you are doing when you enter into this type of agreement.

THE PROPOSAL

A proposal is an informal business document in which you confirm that a meeting was held and work was discussed. When you write up the results of a meeting, the person you met with has an opportunity to pass the information along to someone else and get approval. Having a written document to address increases the likelihood of the initial discussion resulting in work, driving the idea onward into the next phase in the approval process. It should be friendly and informal in tone, but contain specific elements.

It is intended to sound as though it has substance. It should state your capabilities with regard to the client's needs and suggest commitment; contain a review of their needs without committing you to a price; and mention their need to proceed quickly but skip any fees you will charge for changes they make later. Properly written, it is a hook urging them to continue to the letter of intent stage of the process.

THE FORMAT

A cover letter may be a separate introductory page or include all of the remaining elements. The length of the story will be a determining factor. The company on your letterhead should be registered with (depending on local regulations concerning business registration) the town in which your business is located. This should be on a printed company masthead or from a high quality computer printer. The appearance of the document will represent you to persons you have yet to meet and will leave your first impression. It is cliché but still as serious as when it was written: "You never get a second chance to make a first impression."

The company letterhead should contain the company logo. Use the *Prentice Hall Reference Guide to Grammar and Usage* (Muriel Harris, Prentice Hall, 1997) or an equivalent as a guide to proper grammar. Use your spell checker. Proofread your document two or three times, and ask someone to proof it once more. Print it on good bond paper, nothing fancy, no colors. Print the address on the envelope. Many clients keep envelopes for the address. It must look as good as the rest of the document. Use the client's business card to be sure you have the correct spelling of the name. People may discard a letter with their name misspelled because it shows a lack of attention to detail.

Address the letter to the person you spoke with. The first sentence should contain the statement "...to confirm our conversation of Wednesday, January 16, 2000 I am providing the following proposal".

Include three of your business cards with the proposal, one for the person you spoke with first; he may have lost your card between the meeting, his home, and his office. The second will get clipped to the proposal as it is passed around. The third may get passed to a colleague at some later date as a referral if you do a good job.

THE STORY

From the notes you took during your first meeting with the client you must now construct an interesting and detailed story. An outline is always a good idea. It may be one paragraph if the logo is simply to pop onto the screen; it may be a long document if there is a complex series of images to present in the background. Some car ads must take several pages to describe even if they are only 15 seconds long.

There should be no technical terms, use "... an explosion with white glowing sparks emanating from the center" rather than "...break apart the sphere object using the dynamic-explode plug-in with a material glow filter...." Use terms like "...then we get very close to the young woman's eye..." rather than "Cut to an extreme close-up of the actress' left eye...."

It is through the story that you tell the client that you understand his vision of the logo piece. People spend weeks staying up nights designing these pieces. You must put thought into how you are going to present it in 3D. The client wants you to make it look good.

DESCRIPTION OF THE PRODUCT

This is a separate paragraph in which you describe how you are going to deliver the actual finished piece. It might read "...animation to be delivered within five weeks of release of project. It will be delivered to Mr. First Client on one Beta tape containing three consecutive copies with ten seconds of black between each and one additional copy on VHS Gold." This description should be placed after the story.

CREATING A NEED TO ACT

This is the point when you try to get your client to act now; an example would be if you were given information during the initialdiscussion such as "We need to show this piece at the annual event in two months." Your closing sentence should read, "In order to deliver this piece prior to <two months date from now> we will have to begin the construction of the virtual model within three days. By planning ahead you will help us both avoid a rush at the end."

WHAT NOT TO INCLUDE

Do not include a price in this document. If you are specifically asked to include a price, end the bid text with a statement "per your request, pricing will follow immediately in my bid." If you faxed the bid overnight and it is there when the client arrives, you can fax the formal quote at 10:00. The two should not get to the client at the same time.

The bid is intended to be an informal document. It is intended to intrigue, to fire the imagination of the client. It should paint a rosy but accurate picture of the animation. The price should be part of a formal document; including it in the proposal loses opportunities.

Video Magic Presentations

1234 Any Street
Marching, GA 30064
November 1, 2000

Mr. Jack McGillicutty
BSE Electric Conglomerate
1212 West Eastern Street
Atlanta, GA 30066

Dear Mr McGillicutty:

To document the results of our meeting I am presenting the following proposal. By December 1st 2000 we can provide BSE Electric with a 10-second flying logo. The logo will be delivered on VHS tape.

I am proposing that the logo be modeled in 3D using the 2D-art work being prepared by Add-an-Ad Agency of Atlanta as a guide . The screen will be blackened at the start of the piece and the logo will spin from the distance coming toward the viewer until it fills the screen. The image will be of a chargecard-shaped rectangle with the text of BSE, with the crossed double line and five circles design used by the company. The lines and circles will spin and move randomly but travel along with the card shape and the text. All the elements will come together at the last moment of the animation.

Audio will be provided to me on disk in .WAV format. The artwork must arrive at my studio no later than November 5th in order to meet the deadline.

Please confirm by fax that we are in agreement on the content of this proposal, and I will prepare a bid with pricing and more specific information

The proposal for a 30-second commercial reusing the logo at a later date will arrive under separate cover.

Thank you for the opportunity to meet with you about this work.

Sincerely,

Bruce W. Jones

Bruce W. Jones

A simple proposal. The proposal is intended to begin the dialog. It should be all positive, listing benefits, but with very little technical detail. If you get the interest of the client, you will get a chance to bid on the job. If not, create a better proposal next time.

THE BID FORMAT

Like the proposal, the bid should have a cover letter. Address it to the person you first met with or, if directed otherwise (i.e. to an art director or purchasing agent in the company), be certain you have the correct spelling of that person's name. It is considered acceptable business etiquette to call the receptionist of a company and ask for the correct spelling and department of an employee. It should refer to the proposal in the first sentence, such as "...this is to follow up my proposal of <proposal date> about the flying logo animation for <logo name>," or "Thank you for your request for a bid on the logo work proposed <proposal date>..." This cross referencing is to help people who have to file these documents.

THE GOOD STUFF

A short review of the story in one or two sentences, just in case the original proposal has become lost, and for later cross-reference, should be included. A description of the degree of finish to be applied to the story and a time line should be included along with preferred start date, latest possible start date, interim meetings, final approval of animatic, approval prior to final rendering (last date to make changes without late delivery), delivery date and format (restated).

GIVING SEVERAL PRICES

Pricing the job is a difficult process. The price should represent something that has been negotiated and agreed to by both parties, should be fair within the local marketplace, and should give you a profit appropriate to the years of work you have put into learning how to be an animator. You must amortize your overhead and expenses and give the client what their company needs.

Often the acceptance of your price doesn't have much to do with any of these factors. The price tags on your competitor's bids (if any), the amount budgeted for this project (something clients generally will not share with you directly) and how serious the client is about your doing that particular piece all affect pricing.

I use the following method to evaluate work. I ask what, if anything, has been budgeted for the project. I work up a price per second or minute figure based on current market price (often discussed at user group meetings). Then I calculate how long it will take me to create and produce the work being asked for and multiply by my hourly rate and double that figure for overhead. A meeting with an accountant will yield you a much better figure for overhead but double your rate, times the estimated total time to complete, is a close figure.

If those two calculation methods yield something close, then you are close to a good price. If the two methods are significantly different, go with the higher price. It is better to lose a job because of a high bid than to hurt yourself with a low one.

CLEAR TERMS AND CONDITIONS

You must include a cluster of statements about how the work will be defined and specify what remedies will occur if the work expands outside those parameters. What happens if materials promised as reference don't arrive on time? What happens if the design is changed at a later date? What will be the charge if changes occur after you have completed the models? If changes are made after approval of the animatic or proofs, who will cover the costs to make those changes? You should also include a statement about what constitutes a revision.

TERMS OF PAYMENT

Separate from the price are the conditions of payment. When someone finally says, "O.K., let's do it," you shift gears. If you are not present for this event you must provide for the person making the decision to have a way to start the ball rolling. No job has started until money has been exchanged. Most jobs work on a thirds plan: one third to be paid on signing of the contract or at the time of commitment to start the job (the rationale here is that money is needed to cover scanning costs, labor to build the model, photography fees, etc.); the second third is paid upon approval of the preview or animatic (costs of rendering make a second payment practical at this time); and the final third upon delivery.

Never invest in creating the animation portion of the work until you have actually collected the first third. If the deadline is tight and the company needs to have you start the job now, the company can find a way to give you a check now. The final payment must be discussed at the time they accept the job. Some companies pay within 30 days of receipt of invoice, many after 60 days. It is sometimes necessary to present a final bill at the start of the job in order to be paid upon completion. By payment upon completion, I mean you slide the VHS tape across the table and let go of it when their check is in your other hand, and not before. More than once I have showed up at a client's place of business, shown the final version of a tape, gotten approval, asked for payment, been told it would be ready tomorrow and put the tape back into my pocket and picked up my other things to leave. It is amazing how many checks that were going to be ready tomorrow could suddenly be found today when the client wanted the tape today.

THE CLIENT STORYBOARD

There are two general categories of storyboards. The first is the client storyboard prepared for presentation to the client. This is usually created so that it is easily understood by a nonanimator. Make clear drawings of features and characters. Use color where it will enhance rather than distract. Eight to twelve carefully selected frames are usually enough for a sales pitch.

THE FORMAT

There are precut black presentation boards that have openings for the drawings and separate openings for the text. Use them: Cutting your own is not worth the time. Hand letter the text in pencil. It is easier to change on the fly that way. Ink (and, if applicable, color) in marker and pencil (if you have the skills) or hire an artist to draw the storyboard images for you. Mount the pictures, text and presentation frame on 1/4" cardboard or foam-based board for rigidity. Be certain to check that there will be an easel or something similar on which to place your storyboard.

THE TEXT

The text should reflect the story (or the most recent revision of it) presented in the proposal. There should be one or two lines to describe each of the key elements chosen for illustrations. Special effects should be described in nontechnical terms within brackets. Time of each part of the shot should be given in seconds. If you can't print well or neatly, and you don't want to pay someone who can, use an easily read typeface for the text. Make sure the type is big enough or bold enough so you can read it without bending over while you discuss it. If your storyboard spills over onto a second or even third board, practice a method for taking one down and putting the next one up while you are speaking. Nothing is more distracting than a presenter who doesn't know what to do with his props.

WHAT TO INCLUDE

A storyboard is intended to give an outline of the action that will take place during the animation. If your logo is going to spin, draw it with motion lines off the edges and put arrows on it to show which way. If you are not familiar with conventions about how to show the action on a storyboard, refer to *Storyboards, Motion in Art* by Mark Simon (ISBN 1-887118-00-4) for some suggestions. The first and last frames must always be represented, as well as key frames or major transitions, establishing shots, close-ups and for the client, big close-ups of their product or, in this case, logo. In a flying logo the client wants maximum exposure of his company's symbol.

WHAT NOT TO INCLUDE

Do not use balloons, sexual references, religious references, or political references in your illustrations. They are always taboo. The same is true for the text and for your verbal presentation. In your text, do not use SMPTE time codes or frames as time references. Executives do not think in these time standards, only seconds. Do not include software names or plug-in terminology, as these don't mean anything to anyone outside the trade.

CHAPTER 2 PRESENTING YOUR BID

THE PRESENTATION

Shower in the morning, use your dandruff shampoo, dress well, use deodorant, skip the cologne altogether or use it by the drop, not the handful (many people are allergic to it). Bad breath will kill your chances of working with people as fast as a bad story-board. Brush your teeth and 30 minutes before arriving, use breath mints, polish your shoes and comb your hair before walking in the door.

Do all that stuff your mother bothered you about while you were growing up. Do not eat fish, onions, strong cheeses, garlic bread, drink beer or other liquor, or smoke anything before a presentation.

Even though all your meetings so far have been with your now-good friend, Fred the agent, when you arrive to show your storyboard there is frequently a committee. These people want to know what they are getting for the $5,000 price tag you put on that 30 seconds of animation.

Greet each person with a firm but not bone-crushing hand-shake. Look each in the eye and say, "Good to meet you." Learn and use the names of the people you are presenting to; it is appropriate to ask in advance who you will be presenting to and memorize the list of names. Connect the faces to those names when you meet the participants. Pass out business cards to people as you meet them, and take theirs if offered. Place the business cards on the table near where you are to stand while presenting. Lay the cards out in the same pattern as the people are seated; refer to them if you forget someone's name.

Politely refuse mixed drinks, beer or wine; take a soft drink instead, or get a glass of water to put at arm's reach.

You will often meet with a president or CEO; their approval may be required for a large expenditure. Do not put your foot in your mouth. False praise gets you nowhere; a broad smile and an honest "thank you for coming" will go a lot farther. They may not stay longer than the introductions or for the first few minutes of your presentation.

They will be making a judgement about your professionalism and self-confidence. These people have no interest in the specifics. They are asking nonverbal questions, "Does this person know what they are doing, do I trust this person, will this person deliver and follow through or cause us trouble?" They will signal their subordinates with their approval or rejection outside of your field of view. If half the room clears before your presentation is to begin, if you are asked to cut your presentation short, or if you are asked to come back later, drop your storyboard in the trash. You failed the test.

Set up as quickly and efficiently as you can without being rushed. Ask for help moving things if you need it. Be certain you have everything you need before you indicate you are ready to start; use a written checklist if necessary. Chat until someone calls the room to order. This may be an executive seating himself and offering you an open hand as a signal for you to begin, or it may be a formal introduction.

If you have been asked to present video credentials, call ahead to be certain that there is a TV-VCR combo available for you to use. If not beg, borrow, or rent one and make sure it works before you leave to go to your meeting. Practice your introductory line, such as: "Thank you for coming. I have been asked to show some work that is similar to what I will be creating for you. I will be presenting a few minutes of work on tape before I present the storyboard for your new animated logo."

Ask someone in the back of the room to turn off the lights. Start your tape and sit with your back to the audience; if you sit or stand and face them, someone will start asking questions and no one will see the video. Three to five minutes of your work is quite sufficient. Have a line to use to end the presentation politely. Turn the sound down, then off, say something such as "I hope that was entertaining. Are there any questions about any of that work?" As a courtesy, warn people before you flip on the room lights back on. Always answer all questions before going on to the next part of the presentation.

During your verbal presentation do not stick your hands in your pockets, do not scratch yourself or use the expression "um." Skip all slang expressions and all technical terms. Drop any and all exaggerations. Do your presentation before someone who will give you constructive criticism prior to doing it for a business group; it will significantly improve your self-confidence. The idea may have come from the company but the method of presentation is your work. Present it with confidence and pride. If what you have done is good quality, it will get a good response.

When you are done say "Thank you for your attention. Are there any comments or questions?" Do not answer questions with apologies and do not become defensive. These people may have a better view of the market than you do. They are primarily interested in their company's success, and you should be also.

Take notes on people's comments. Some will be significant and affect the course of the job. Some people just feel a need to share their observations but need not be reacted to. Thank everyone for their comments. Answer any technical questions in nontechnical terms, being careful not to be condescending or talk below anyone's level of intelligence. You should have been able to draw some conclusions about the technical expertise level of the people at the meeting during the initial chat period.

It should be easy to tell when the meeting is drawing to a close. Never appear to be in a hurry to leave. Pick up slowly. Some people will want to talk to you privately. They are embarrassed to ask questions before a group, or may be aware their question doesn't have universal appeal. It is important to stay and talk to these people. Some quiet people who stay after meetings are the technical advisors who have a guiding, rather than a loud, influence on the company.

HANDLING THE LARGE COMMITTEE

Large groups often turn into discussion sessions. Always listen carefully and take notes. Many good suggestions may arise. Avoid camps forming and watch for the formation of splinter groups who begin to defend an idea. "Let's keep brainstorming before we lock into any ideas" can often open the discussion up again.

Again, don't commit to changes; say "...that is worth considering..." and discuss it with your contact person later as to how you need to respond. You may have to call or meet a second time with an individual with a strong point of view and negotiate on some points.

THE CLOSE

Determining when agreement has been reached will vary almost by the situation. If the CEO stays through your presentation, a comment "...wonderful, let's proceed with this..." is enough to secure the job as presented. Other times protracted discussions are needed. Always remind everyone holding up the process that the deadline for final changes is approaching. If negotiations continue to the drop-dead date, be clear that negotiations must end or the job must be withdrawn. Most people get off the fence at this time. Always appear to be the patient individual waiting for everyone else to reach agreement. Never lose your temper.

AFTERWARDS

Request a meeting with your contact as soon as possible to review the storyboard presentation. A phone conversation is sometimes sufficient if the animation is simple and the questions are few. Ask your contact about which of the comments he feels you need to respond or reply to. Are any changes required, or can you proceed?

THE CONTRACT

The question about whether a contract is needed or not is open to debate. In favor of a contract, its writing brings clarity to the job. If a great deal of money is involved, for example over $25,000, it may be in order for the protection of both parties. On the other hand, writing a contract can be expensive and time consuming. Most attorneys ask $150 per hour and more for this type of work. If you get a purchase order number for the job, it is a binding contract in most situations. If you get one third down payment, an additional third about halfway through the job, and don't deliver the finished tape without leaving with a check, how can you get burned?

YOU AND YOUR ATTORNEY

An attorney can help you avoid a lot of trouble by pointing out the pitfalls of your enthusiastic plans to jump into things you know nothing about. Contracts, finance, copyrights, ownership and many other rights and responsibilities should be discussed with your attorney. What is best for the short term may not always be the safest business strategy. Incorporation may work better for some than others. Liability and insurance should be discussed as well.

CLAUSES AND CONDITIONS

You should bring special clauses and conditions that relate to animation to the attention of your attorney. Without expensive investigation, attorneys can not be expected to be aware of those problems and pitfalls peculiar to this industry.

Time-related problems are paramount on your list of concerns. Animation work requires unusually tight planning. Reference materials arriving late or design or color changes to the model after specific dates may make the project impossible to deliver or significantly more expensive. Penalties and remedies for such failures should be stated in the contract. Cancellation in mid-project after approval of the storyboard but before the animatic is presented, or after the animatic but before the frames have been rendered, should be considered.

REVISIONS

Milestone points in your timeline that could be affected by late arrival of information or changes to the design of the product:

1. drawings, comps, or physical models that have to be scanned and that are required to start the building of the 3D model

2.   color, size, or relational information concerning the use of the logo per the legal description of that logo

3.   extensive changes made after viewing the animatic

4.   changes requested after the start of the final rendering to frames

5.   failure to provide the music or voice-over/script on time

6.   problems with output to the final format

A timeline of the entire project should be created as an exercise before presenting the bid to the client. The timeline should be worked backwards from the requested delivery date and should serve as theoretical proof that the project can be delivered on the proposed date.

When possible, the timeline should be put together and/or reviewed by key members of the animation staff, not just your sales person. Seemingly small details can sometimes adversely impact delivery times. Try, through exhaustive discussion, to work through all possible situations that could affect delivery.

An entirely different timeline may be put together after the bid has been secured for use in defining the responsibilities of the various people involved in the actual production phase. At this level, model builders, materials, lighting and camera specialists should work with cinema people (if any video must be shot) and the final editors to come to agreement about scheduling. This group must consider the need for additional in-house people or contracting outside your studio.

REALISTIC ESTIMATES

Let's say that you have been asked to produce a very simple logo piece: one symbol, a standard typeface requiring no modification of the letter shapes, background to be a bright blue sky, the logo color a standard Pantone color that falls well within the NTSC color capabilities spectrum, simple motion, one spotlight to pan across the face of the text, and 30 seconds in length. Not too much can go wrong with a project like this.

The model can be built, the colors applied, the light set up and animated in a single day. The frames can be run out overnight (900 of them at about 10 seconds each = 9,000 seconds/60sec/min = 150 minutes or less than 3 hours' rendering time). The delivery date is five days. All is well. You see this client as a potential person who can provide more work in the future. You want to bid it as low as possible but not create a perception of buying in.

If the going rate for an average animation in your area is $5,000/minute, $2,500 would seem a fair price. Calculated at 12 hours of work at $200/hour, we come up with a similar figure and it would appear realistic. If you were to bid this job at $2,000 you would be the low bidder and probably assure yourself the job.

ALLOWING FOR THE UNEXPECTED

Let's imagine that you succeeded in completing the model and set up for animation and your system crashed. The shop wanted three days to rebuild the ramcharger capacity chip. The client calls and tells you that they would like to have you meet with them on the fourth day instead of the fifth with the animation complete, because their client has moved up the schedule. They also want you to bid on another, larger project due on the same date. You have three choices:

1. you can turn them down (bad idea, but always an option)
2. you can try to buy, assemble, and load the software onto a new computer, capable of outputting to tape, and still try to render the project in house (it is unlikely you will get it to run correctly in time and it will cost you $12,000 or so)
3. you can call a friend and pay him/her to render it for you at the going rate (about $1/frame)

The last is a good solution; however, look at what you have done to your profit. Where $2,400 to $2,500 may have seemed sufficient initially, it is now eaten up in costs and overhead, and the $/hour rate for your working time is well below your expected minimum.

TESTING YOUR FRAMES

Students frequently do something that professionals don't: When the model is completed and lights, cameras, special effects, etc., are done they set the machine to render and leave.

Professionals put in the hour or more necessary to run the rendering in preview mode. This mode allows you to view a monochromatic version of the animation. Make a last check on the timing and give a look-see to be sure nothing passes in front of something else unexpectedly.

Another thing that professionals do is to set the rendering to every tenth or so frame and sit in front of the monitor and watch those random frames render into thin air. This procedure allows you, the artist, to look for unexpected shifts in color, a blocked light from

something off stage casting a stray shadow, or an inverted face you hadn't noticed before. (With release 3.1 of MAX you can keep those frames and MAX will recognize their existence and render only the fill-in frames required.)

REALISTIC ESTIMATION OF YOUR HARDWARE CAPABILITIES

While those random frames are rendering, note the rendering times. Times per frame will vary across an animation; making an estimate of rendering time from the first frame is a dangerous and deceptive way of guestimating. You should take the longest frame time that turned up and multiply that by the total number of frames to get the actual rendering time.

CHAPTER 3 CREATING THE ANIMATION FOR THE FLYING LOGO

THE ANIMATION

The animation has six separate parts:

1. Building the model and setting up the environment

Text or simple geometric forms constitute the volume of model building involved in flying logo projects. Frequently the company advertising department will provide you with "comps" of the company logo. These comps are extremely fine resolution printouts of the text and/or company symbol which you can scan for tracing. Smaller companies will give you a business card or printed letterhead as an example. Sometimes small company owners will work with an ad agency that has the comps, but the owner doesn't know to offer them to you; be sure to ask. You must also ask if the comps need to be returned. When they have to be returned, be extremely careful to handle them by the edges only so that you do not fingerprint them.

2.   Placing materials on the model (and backgrounds)

Materials are created in MAX in the Materials Editor. Many of these contain maps or picture files of actual materials. Many of these materials are provided by the client to you as physical samples. You get the image of the sample into the Material Editor by scanning it. How to scan it—file size, color depth, file format, external annotation, naming conventions, and choice of compression technique–could be a whole book. Materials scaling and proper application can make or break your illustration or animation.

3. Lighting the model and the environment

There are several lighting options in MAX. Selecting the right one will enhance your image dramatically. Since in most cases, the materials on a logo are simple ones, lighting them to best advantage is important. Knowing how light affects real objects will make you better at this part of the job. Experts in lighting work for lighting firms or as photographers; they have learned to sculpt the world out of light. Classes in photographic lighting of architectural interiors and exteriors will improve your expertise.

4.   Setting up cameras in relation to the models

You are the cameraman. Understanding camera settings, lenses, types of shots and camera locations and angles used to lend pathos or drama are skills worth studying and mastering. Taking a class in video camera use and in video editing will make you conscious of the needs of editors when you have to produce animation or stills for their use.

5.   Animating the models in the scene and/or the cameras

The ability to set up smooth camera paths or add fractalized movement to a camera's path are skills that you need to know how to apply. The animation of objects and creatures are additional skill sets to be mastered. Entire books have been written on the how-to of animation. Every situation calls for a different controller or dummy attachment, linking technique or inverse kinematic trick. The more of these tricks you can master and put into your bag of tricks, the better animator you will be.

6.   Video post processing (f/x and output)

More special effects are called for in logo work by the science fiction film industry than anyone else. At this time, there are more than 150 free plug-ins available on the Web and better than 50 retail packages offering some type of add-on to the standard MAX package. Most of these are there to blow up, add a glow, more sparks, lightning, dust, scratches, and more to your animation or illustration after you have finished its basic construction.

Special effects lose their "special" characteristic when over used. They are intended to be used as spice. Special effects can be added in the Video Post processor, within MAX at rendering, or added after you have completed your work in MAX by using programs such as Adobe After f/x or Speed Razor. Cuts and transitions such as cross-fades or blends can be accomplished in many different ways as well.

Output is decided between you and the client or the client's editor. Never go past the proposal stage in negotiations without determining the output format expected. An .AVI file made for CD use renders faster than the .TGA files required for near broadcast quality video from a Personal Video Recorder based system. Output on 1" digital tape or for film requires expensive equipment and extremely large format files. The models used for these media are higher resolution as well.

These six steps have to be carried out, usually in this order, to complete any animation project. Let's look at the process and order of operations for the actual creation of the animation.

LOGO CONTENT

A text-only logo is unusual. There is often a symbol or a by-line associated with the text symbol. The relationship of these elements is often dictated by the legal description of the logo and must be adhered to. The typeface of the by-line may also be dictated. Never forget that the client is interested in his logo being the most important piece on the screen. Fill the screen with it as often as possible.

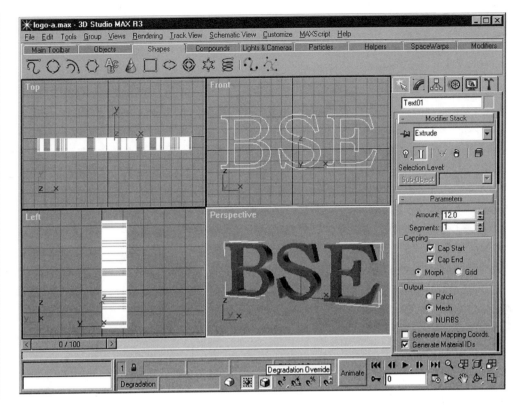

This is basic text created in 3D Studio MAX 3.0. It is a two-step process involving the creation of the text as a 2D shape. It is then extruded into the third dimension.

TYPEFACE

You start by choosing the typeface for your logo text. If you're fortunate enough to have the client tell you what the typeface is, you are already part way home. Usually you have to carefully observe the text, and depending on your expertise and experience with text, simply match the typeface by observation. Look for overall characteristics, width of horizontals vs. verticals, serif vs. sans serif (little extra tails or capitals and bases vs. the more simplified forms). Observe both upper and lower case; some will only match in the upper. Be aware that some are simply custom and will have to be traced or otherwise reconstructed (see later in this section on tracing custom text).

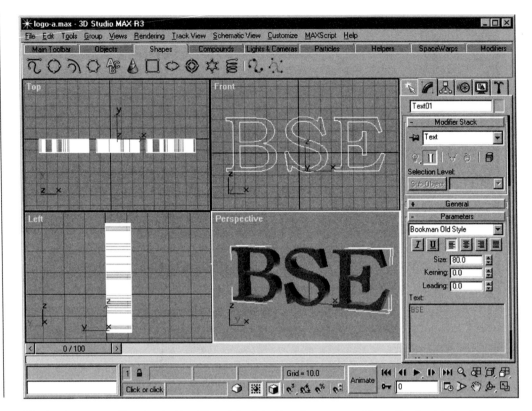

The basic screen with extruded text. The default text has been overwritten with client text; change the typeface and the text will change to reflect that.

IMPORTING TEXT

Text that is not directly available in 3D Studio MAX can sometimes be loaded where MAX can access it. For format reasons, that text which is not possible to import can often be set in other vector-based programs and exported in a format MAX can read. Adobe Illustrator or Corel Draw are good sources for typefaces. .AI or .DXF are good export/import formats; .EPS works when these fail with secondary interpreters such as AutoCAD in between.

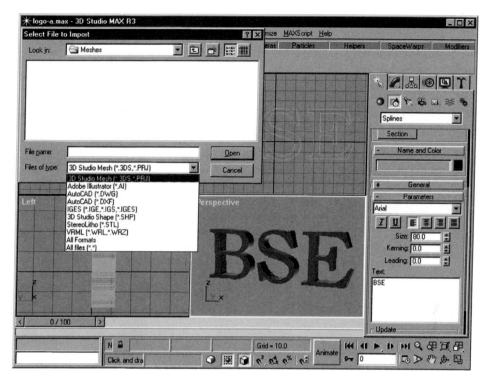

The import selection window, showing the various import formats available.

INITIAL TEXT

The size of the text will not make any difference unless it is in a relationship with additional elements. When that is the case you must be aware of the size value shown in the dialog box. The size is given in points. Points are a printer's unit of measurement. Unless you are familiar with this system, you will probably want to convert to decimals or fractions.

There are 96 points to the inch. The following chart will give you some numbers to extrapolate from in the future.

EQUIVALENTS:

POINT SIZE	DECIMAL	FRACTION
4	.060	(1/16)
6	.078	(5/64)
8	.094	(3/32)
10	.109	(7/64)
12	.125	1/8
14	.156	(5/16)
18	.219	(7/32)
24	.250	1/4
30	.281	(9/32)
36	.313	(5/16)
42	.375	3/8
48	.500	1/2
60	.625	5/8
72	.750	3/4
84	.875	7/8
96	1.000	1
120	1.188	(13/16)
180	1.750	1 3/4

(—)=rounded

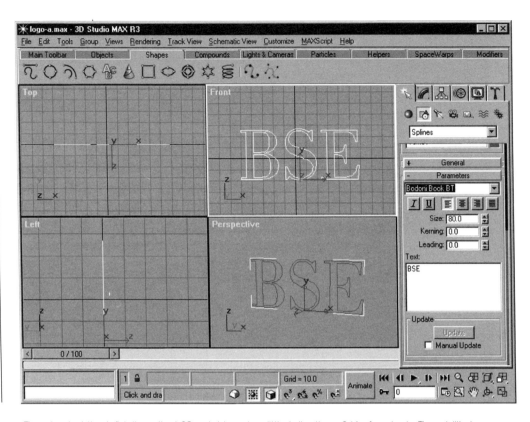

The chart at the left tells us that 80 point type is a little taller than 3/4 of an inch. The ability to convert decimals to fractions (and back) is a skill you should cultivate.

ADDING THICKNESS

This step was accomplished by choosing the EXTRUDE button. How much extrude is good? I have found that when the thickness of extrusion matches the wide element of the text, .ie., width = thickness, the text can be read most clearly and is visually pleasing. Text that is too thin doesn't give you an opportunity to use the strength of good solid objects. Overly thick text doesn't read well. It becomes distracting, looks forced and exaggerated.

Radiused and chamfered (clipped) corners can be accomplished by LOFTing and using the FIT/DEFORM features rather than using EXTRUDE. This adds significantly to the polygon count (overall file size) and is usually more distracting than valuable.

Radii on edges are most valuable when the text is intended to have a metallic material or is intended to look old and worn, such as old stone.

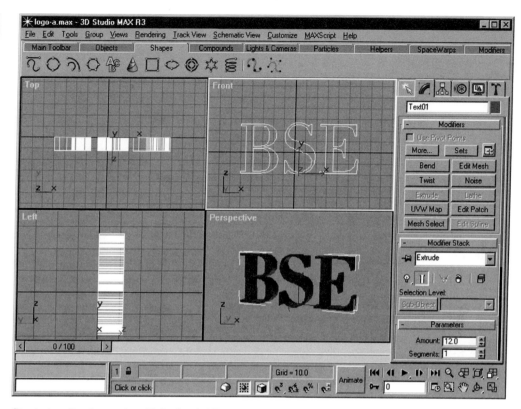

The text outline becoming 3D for the first time.

SUPPORTING ELEMENTS

The block of material in the back of the text, the "card" shape, could have been created with the OBJECT PRIMITIVE/BOX command. The size of the CHAMFER BOX, like the simple box, can be read directly in the dialog boxes below the main window (just below the window shown in the illustration). If we had begun here, we would have had to do a great deal of additional work to round all the corners. The choice of the EXTENDED PRIMITIVES/CHAMFER BOX allows us to do both operations at once.

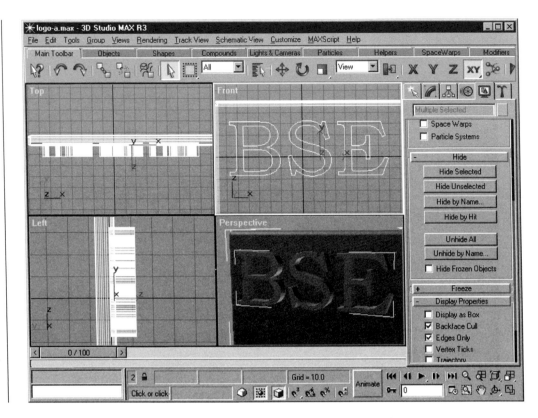

The choice here of a PRIMITIVE BOX or a CHAMFER BOX can save labor later.

INTERACTIVE MODIFICATION

By switching to the modify window while the CHAMFER BOX is still selected, you can change the number of segments and smooth the corners of the box interactively.

After additional operations have been performed on the box, it becomes necessary to work your way down the stack to the step prior to where the modification took place. Be certain that your modification of the basic shape does not adversely affect later changes (higher up the chain of modifications).

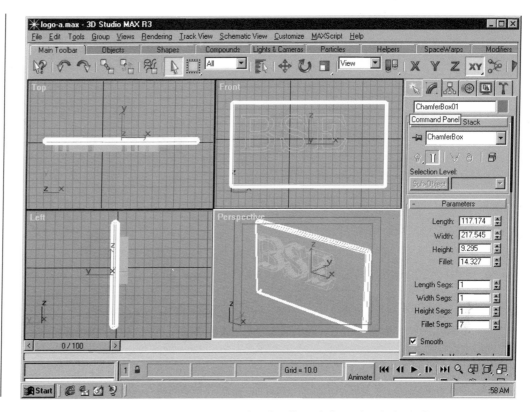

By switching to the extended primitives and using the ChamferBox extended primitive you can save a lot of work later (doing Boolean operations or fit/deforms) by creating a backdrop object with rounded edges, all at the same time.

ADDITIONAL ELEMENTS

Simple rectangular shapes with sharp corners are BOX PRIMITIVES. After creating one horizontal or vertical, use the SELECT, MOVE tool with the shift key depressed to make three additional copies.

Select two of the copies, lock in the rotation, and rotate 90 degrees. The two vertical elements should be shorter and can be made shorter in one of several ways. The easiest way to shorten them is to use the MODIFY pull-down with the object selected and reduce its height by sliding the spinner next to its height value.

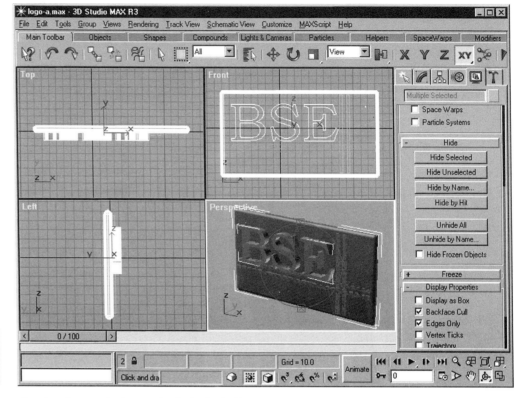

By using the regular box and cylinder tools (shown next illustration), you can create the rest of the structure of the 3D card look.

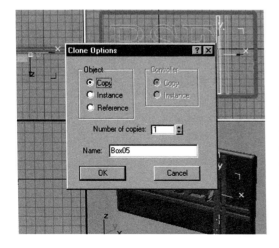

When you have created one vertical element and want to create a second of exactly the same size, choose the move key and hold down the shift key. When you move an object with the shift key down, it opens this dialog box on your screen. Copy makes an independently editable copy of the original; Instance makes a clone; Reference makes a clone that is bidirectionally variable. You can accept the default name or give the new object one of your own (usually the better idea).

SECONDARY TEXT

Secondary text is usually created in the same typeface, but smaller. It often combines upper and lower case. The location of pieces of text and their spatial relationship may be dictated by copyright specifications. Check with the person in the company responsible for maintaining the logo or the attorney who created the specification before doing any final work on any design involving a logo or trademark.

The other elements can be sunk into the surface of the backdrop to decrease their importance if necessary. Once the parts have been placed as you want them in relationship to each other, you can join them by selecting them all, then using the group pull-down option and giving them an easily identifiable name, such as "cardparts."

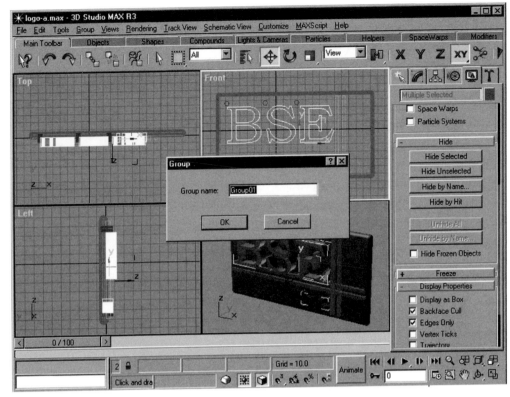

The thickness of the secondary text should less than the thickness of the primary text.

Grouping makes the parts easier to move together later. This is the group dialogue box; enter a name for your grouped objects.

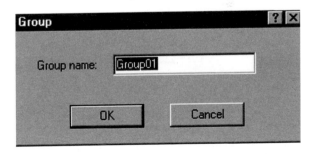

FULL VIEW

Frequently view your handiwork full screen before proceeding. Use the rotate view button and switch between the USER VIEW and PERSPECTIVE VIEW.

To switch between these VIEWS, make sure the view you want to switch to is selected (use your right mouse key to select without losing your selected items) and use the U and P hot keys.

The large text and the horizontal bars are too close. It is best to correct this now, when you see it for the first time. After a while you will overlook it and forget to correct the problem.

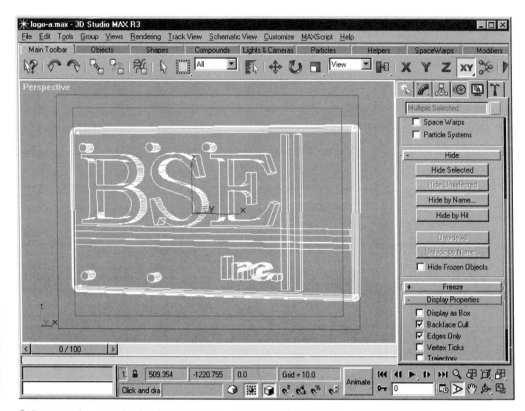

Full screen views are the best way to review your work. Switch frequently and correct errors as you work. Don't leave them until later; you will get used to seeing them and after a while you will not see them at all.

REFERENCE MATERIAL

Sometimes the only reference material you receive is a photograph, sketch, or a sample such as a business card or letterhead. When this is what you have to work from, start by scanning the original in a high resolution (i.e., 300 dpi or higher) full color format.

By scanning the file on a flat bed scanner you will eliminate as much distortion as possible. If you don't want to purchase a scanner, most service bureaus will scan pictures for you (for a fee, of course). The cost of commercial scanning can be reduced by bringing your own disk and specifying that you want a file size selected that will fill the disk. For a black and white scan of a business card, a floppy is sufficient. For a highly detailed or full color 8" x 10" image you will want a 24 bit, 300 dpi file which will take up 80 or more meg of space and will require a ZIPcartridge. Most service bureaus have ZIP drives but you must ask if they have a PC format ZIP—there is also a MAC version.

The file of the scan, once created, should be treated with the same care you would use to handle any archival document. Make back-up copies on various media. If you had it scanned by a service bureau onto a floppy, back it up on your hard drive before you begin working with it.

If the client provides a hand sketch, it can be traced and then brought up in Corel Photo Paint or Adobe PhotoShop and resampled to a smaller, more convenient size. Custom text like this will not lend itself to matching an existing typeface. If the logo has a symbol or icon that is to be done in 3D, it too will have to be traced.

BLOW-UPS

It is helpful to have close-ups of your file. If the original is scanned at 600 d.p.i, you can do a large, detailed blow-up to make the tracing process easier.

Tracing is done with the LINE (spline) tool in MAX. If you choose to trace in AutoCAD, use the PLINE/PEDIT/SMOOTH combination or SPLINE tool. Experiment with each and you will find advantages of both, depending on the circumstances.

Another option is to use the SPLINE tools in Corel Draw or Adobe Illustrator. Once the trace is done in either, proceed to .DXF it out and back into MAX and EXTRUDE or LOFT. The AUTOTRACE features in each of these programs can speedthe process even more. Be sure you understand the autotrace options. With the various options you can control the number of control points very precisely.

I have begun directly in MAX with an arbitrarily chosen letter. By selecting points around the perimeter, I can define each shape very quickly. The number of points required will be determined by the output you are shooting for at the end. An animation created for the Web will be in the vicinity of 160 × 120 × 72 dpi, often 16 color maximum. This takes a very small file. If the final output is to film, around 4096 × 1862 × 24 bit color (16.7 million colors), hundreds of faces per curve may be required in order to make it look smooth on screen.

Once the convenient parts have been clipped from the scanned photograph, it is ready to be traced.

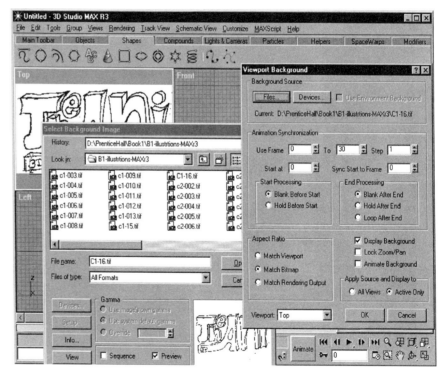

Use the render/environment/ background option, the clipped images can be brought in as a background and traced using the 2D shape/line tool.

THE FLEXIBLE SPLINE

The SPLINE curve is very flexible. Its handles and control points can be manipulated with a high degree of precision. Sometimes, when the form is purely or at least partly geometric, it is easier to start with a circle or square.

Time spent learning about the math behind, and the geometry that can be created by using various types of curves (including the B-spline), will make you a more knowledgeable and effective model builder.

Time spent carefully sculpting these shapes up front will produce the best looking results at rendering.

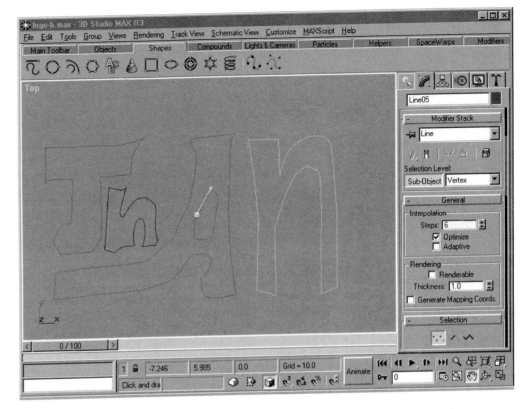

By using the line tool and Edit Spline modifiers you can achieve any level of precise tracing you need. Sometimes it is convenient to include other 2D shapes such as circles and rectangles in the process when parts of letters are very geometric.

SPLINE REVISIONS

When a shape does not drop into place exactly as you want it to, editing is a simple matter of opening the modification pull-down, selecting EDIT SPLINE, selecting the part (s) of the SPLINE to be edited, and right clicking the mouse (with the cursor over the part to be edited).

Each of the optional modifiers will affect each of the sub-object levels differently. VERTEX, SEGMENT, and SPLINE have different options in this window. Familiarize yourself with these options to be efficient with the spline curve.

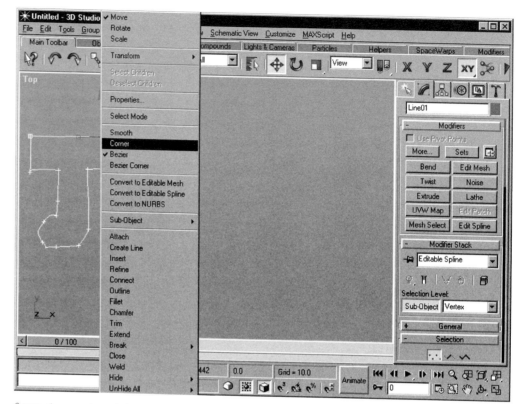

Some shapes do not drop in exactly as you would like. Secondary editing is done with the right click accessible dialog box shown.

CLOSING THE SPLINE

All shapes to be extruded should be closed. When the last point has been selected around the perimeter, pick the first point again and if you are close enough, a dialog box will pop up on the screen and ask you to confirm closing the spline curve.

This act will sometimes produce undesirable results in the form of a lump or distortion at that point. MODIFY/EDIT SPLINE/VERTEX is your best option to reform the last corner and segment shapes.

NOTE: You can extrude the spline without closing it but the Z-normals will not necessarily face outward and your part may appear to vanish. The solution to this (other than closing the spline) is to use a double-sided material on the extruded part.

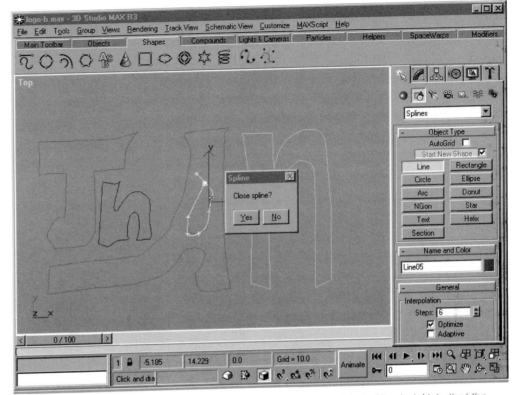

By tracing each element carefully you can reproduce the look and feel of the text. Note that the center of the "A" will have a point on top. This can be removed after closing the spline.

BACKGROUND BY VIEWPORT

Note that the Viewport Background window has a DISPLAY BACKGROUND option check box. With this check box you can turn the background on and off at will. Using this in conjunction with the VIEWPORT box makes it possible to place a different image in each box. This technique is useful when you need to reference photographs of real environments to virtual objects that you may want to integrate into these environments.

Perspective matching features in MAX 3.0 allow a virtually perfect match between your camera view and an existing photograph or animation. The technique of camera matching is well demonstrated on the video provided to all MAX 2.5 owners.

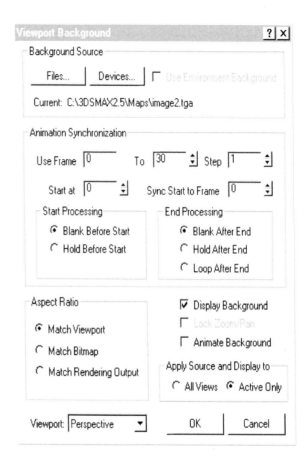

Once all the text has been traced, the background can be shut off using the view/background toggle.

COMPLETE TRACING

The tracing of the first portion of the sketch is complete. The text is a close copy of the original sketch. Each letter is a different color because MAX will assign a new color to each shape as it is created.

It is time to extrude the text. Choose MODIFY EXTRUDE and enter a numeric value or visually establish a depth using the amount spinner.

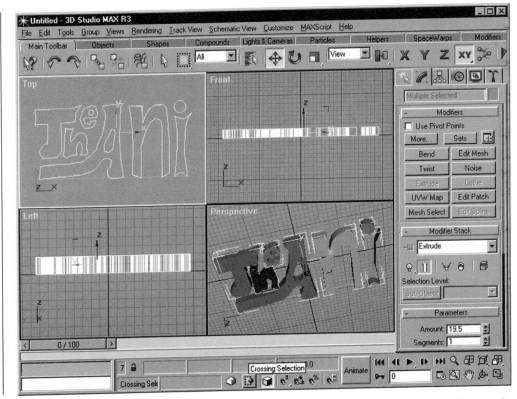

The background has been shut off. The text is now ready for extrusion or further manipulation to refine its shapes.

FINISHED TEXT

Notice the top of the letter "n." It is approximately square, and the letters are not too thick or too thin. Visually pleasing proportions are very important on such a simple assignment.

Depending on the client's vision of the logo you may be all done when you have finished the rest of the tracing. Most likely there is a color used by the company that will be added using the MATERIALS EDITOR.

Add a simple camera. Add whatever animation is in your contract. Render an .AVI file PREVIEW and show it to the client. This is the last chance to make changes without incurring further expense.

Choose a file name that will be easy to remember. If the format is videotape, render the scene to sequentially numbered .TGA (Targa) files. Send them directly to your animation recording device and then out to tape.

Deliver the tape, collect your money.

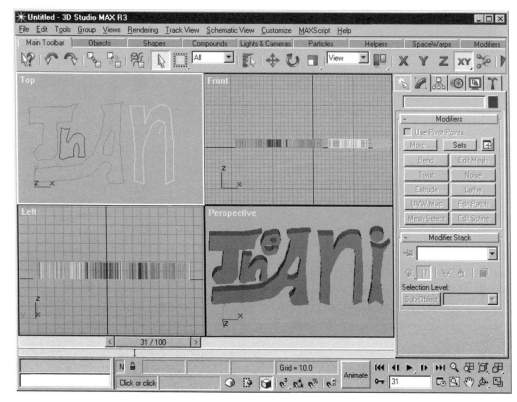

The text has been extruded. Despite the fact that the individual letters are different colors in the window, they can be made the same using the materials editor shown next.

RESOURCES

Typefaces come with most major word processing packages. Illustrator and Corel Draw come with many more. Packages containing new styles are offered everywhere. Trade publications, flyers picked up at industry shows, and mail pieces are all good sources. Building and maintaining a library of type faces can save you a lot of time if you are aware of what you have. Don't get caught in the collectors category where you have 50,000 typefaces and can't find a specific one you need.

Chapter 4 Materials and Lighting

If the company has not trademarked its logo, this is an unregistered product. If the text is being used to announce a seminar or program, the title of which is not a registered trademark, then you have broader freedom to create materials. A lumber company would be a good opportunity to use wood. A hardware store would be a natural candidate for chrome or brass. Be careful of brick, unless you are willing to model each brick. Even with a bump map applied, in close-up it may look phony. Glass, transparent plastics, and ice can also be a problem. You can create visual confusion if you use too many highly reflective surfaces. Over-lapping edges and the multiple planes that become visible through transparent text will impair the reader's ability to grasp the message–you lose the quick read of a logo.

Stock Images: Pro and Con

You can become embroiled in arguments about stock photography. Images, generic or very specific, all of varying degrees of quality, can be purchased from stock houses or distributors as well as (very conveniently) off the Web.

There is heated debate about the sale of these images ruining the photography trade, diminishing the quality of art, about art directors using these relatively inexpensive images to reduce prices of the work of the photographer artist. Do not use photos or copy other art without written permission or paying a release fee to the artist. You can be held liable for misuse.

Lighting Considerations

Conservative businesses such as banks and large firms want conservative lighting. New businesses, small dealerships, and start-ups want glaring spotlights. Exceptions sometimes can be found in television advertising where there is something to be said about flares and glitter on a simple metallic logo or an immobile car to give elegance to an otherwise mundane subject.

In the final analysis we sculpt with light. It can't make a poor model look great, but proper lighting can bring a good model to life.

Camera Techniques

Since the invention of the pin-hole camera, photographers and cinematographers have developed techniques to add various effects to an image. Composition, contrast in value, placement of the center of interest, and viewing angle all add to the overall message an image conveys.

Time spent studying famous films and, more recently, videos of the work of contemporary animators and illustrators is invaluable. Contemporary art has a huge influence on what is popular in illustration as well.

Special Effects, by Hand vs. Plug-Ins

It is always tempting to see new plug-ins and want to own and experiment with them. As a business person you must always look at the cost in relation to what you can justify in terms of the need for the software. Will a job you have now be enhanced or be completed more quickly by buying this software?

Many times the same solution can be obtained by hand, using paint software or using free or inexpensive plug-ins available on the Net.

Output

Once the modeling, materials, lighting, animation, special effects and output to compressed. TGA (for VHS or more demanding formats) has been completed, you will need a method to get the files from the computer to the final medium.

The best cost/value device on the market today for VHS is the Perception Video Recorder® system by Digital Processing, Inc. This hardware is easy to install. The software has an extremely simple interface and allows for a limited amount of video editing and compositing at a reasonable cost.

Format

Various output formats are available for various forms of presentation. Compressed .AVI and .MOV and similar formats are best for CD-based presentations and Web use, while VHS tape is best for boardroom presentations and as a backdrop for speakers. Some work will become part of other edited work and must be done on BETA, BETA-SP or even digital, as in the case of film and some television use.

It is essential that you discuss and confirm the format before bidding the job. Confirm equipment availability.

Time to Completion

Test the frame generation time frequently during the creation process. Many special effects can change the rendering time from several minutes to several hours with the flick of a slider. Testing constantly and doing the math on the total rendering time will keep your schedule grounded in reality.

Late Revisions: Don't Scrap the Whole Thing

It is undesirable but certainly common for a client to ask for a revision at the last minute, often too late to rerender the entire piece. First look carefully at the revision to see how much of the total rendering it affects. Sometimes only those frames or scenes where the change is evident have to be redone. In some cases the change can be done by hand if you have the skills with a paint package or it may be possible to add information later using the post processor and overlaying information onto existingfile sequences.

CHAPTER 5 DELIVERY AND FOLLOW-UP

DELIVERY OF THE PRODUCT

ON-SITE PRESENTATION

I always hand deliver my work personally. I want to be there to present my work and to collect my money. There should be no surprises by this time: You will have shown the preview to the client and gotten a sign-off along the way on materials and background. Occasionally parties in a company show up at the final presentation and make uncomplimentary reviews. Be prepared for these people with responses such as, "I could have made that modification a month ago, but I am afraid it is too late now that the work is completed." Or "Before I leave, I would be happy to give you an estimate of what it would cost to redo the work with that revision; of course it will no longer be delivered on time."

CLIENT WANTS TO COME TO YOUR PLACE

Some people feel uneasy about having a client come to their home office or one-man studio. Many clients, particularly older ones feel a need to have a visual image to connect with a person they work with. I never refuse that need.

I can only recommend cleaning up any mess and putting away any proprietary materials belonging to other clients—though it doesn't hurt to have evidence of other jobs you are working on.

PRESENTING TO A GROUP YOU HAVEN'T MET

At times you may be a subcontractor to another contractor, e.g., you may be producing the animation sequence that becomes part of a video being presented by an architectural firm to an end client who is building a facility. In this case and under any circumstances where you are presenting to an unfamiliar group, ask your client to familiarize you with them as much as possible and make you aware of the interrelationship of all parties involved so you don't put your foot in your mouth.

One important point: Never discuss your fee with anyone else involved in the deal; it will only cause trouble.

COLLECTING YOUR MONEY

If the final tape leaves your hands and you do not walk away with the final payment, for whatever reason, you may have a problem. Laws vary widely from state to state concerning your payment as a business, contractor, subcontractor and as a work for hire employee. Take the time to educate yourself about your state.

There are various ways to collect your money, depending on the amount of money involved. Small claims court has a ceiling on the amount you can apply to collect without an attorney present; learn what it is in your area.

The American Arbitration Association is a group that makes judgments about collection and other disputes between parties. If you include their clause in your agreement, their decision is binding in a court of law.

BACKING-UP

How valuable is your data? Can you afford to lose the model after two weeks of work and still make your deadline? Can you afford to lose your entire materials library that you spent an entire afternoon scanning and editing?

The answer to these questions is always no. There are many back-up systems on the market ranging from the back-up utility that comes with Windows to sophisticated RAID, stripe sets, and mirror or duplicating systems that write two copies of everything you save to two different drives at the same time.

HOW MANY COPIES?

Backing-up your data is important. Back it up twice and take a second copy to a different location, away from your computer.

WHERE?

Theft, robbery, flood and fire are all things that can't be anticipated; things we all assume will not happen to us, but they do happen. I mail my back-ups to a friend out of state; that may be a little paranoid, but I can't afford to lose any of my work.

HOW LONG MUST YOU KEEP THIS STUFF?

Clients sometimes call years after you have completed a job to ask for a second copy or a variation on work you have already done. Most work is so specific you can't reuse much of it so when a client does call for another copy of an old job you are at liberty to charge them for the work again. I keep everything I have done forever; most of the work I archive on ZIP disks because I have found tape back-ups unreliable.

Chapter 6 Prepare for the Next Job

Asking for More Work

A standard business rule of thumb states that 90 percent of your work comes from 10 percent of your clients, and 90 percent of your new business will come from previous clients. I stop in to visit any client I have not heard from in 90 days. I don't stop in to be pushy; I simply stop in to talk and frequently walk away with business. It is not always major, but a situation where subcontracting work to me will make that client's life a little easier, and I have made myself available.

It is considered good business to end each transaction with "Thank you gentlemen. Is there anything more I can do for you at this time?"

Asking for Referrals

I frequently ask my clients, "Has anyone seen that last piece I did for you?" and follow the answer with, "Did they express any interest in having work done for themselves?" If so, "Would you mind sharing their number with me?"

There is no better business than a word-of-mouth referral to a client who has already seen and been impressed by your work. Half the sales pitch is already done for you.

Using a Tickler File

A tickler file is a program or well organized client file system that you can roll over regularly to remind you of who you haven't worked with for a while. All salesmen have a file of potential or existing clients that they check regularly. Many times it is the salesman who is "there" who gets the job.

The Holiday Card

It amazes me that no matter how many business cards I leave with a customer, they call on December 22 after receiving my holiday card and say, "I'm so glad you sent that card, I have work for you and couldn't find your phone number." Baffles me every time.

Holiday cards can work for you if they are chosen well and backfire if they are not. Hand-painted cards with a very simple message, signed personally, are safe.

JOB 2 THE MECHANICAL DEVICE

OBJECTIVE

Create first an image of the product, a hand drill, for advertising to use in sales promotions; second to create an animation to teach manufacturing personnel how to assemble the product; third to expand that animation to include footage of the device operating for additional client presentations.

The mechanical engineering, manufacturing and product assembly portion of the computer illustration and animation market has been growing slowly for many years. Form, fit, and function studies of complex mechanisms and ergonomic use studies can all be enhanced through the use of computer graphics.

Mechanical engineers, like architects, have traditionally built prototypes and test models to review and study the form, fit, and function of their creations. The model builders who create these models, the time involved and the expense of the materials have often stopped experimentation that would have made a better product in the end.

With the advent of 3D modeling it became possible to build models of the machine, check the interaction of moving parts, check for the fit of assembled parts, and to see if the assembly were mechanically possible.

Marketing people discovered long ago that they could use the pictures generated by the engineering department to begin to sell products to their markets without the item ever having been created.

Manufacturing began to study models as a method of pre-training their personnel in anticipation of the arrival of new parts. Pictures of the assembly could be broken down into subassemblies and virtually staged for production.

When engineers began to hire animators to study the movements of parts in machinery, they often found interference that would have caused expensive damage to prototypes. They also found improper fit of parts, and hardware that was impossible to assemble. Money saved and shorter production cycles made this review popular with engineering and management alike.

The manufacturing market doesn't know much about animation. Most of those I have sold work to thought animation meant Saturday morning cartoons. Converts come slowly but steadily; education is the key to moving them toward providing solutions to their problems through animation.

Be prepared to spend a lot of time working through explanations of product function and terminology you may have to ask about more than once. Engineers are meticulous people who move very slowly. They use tools such as ProEngineer and Mechanical Desktop that may require some fancy translation to get the models into a form you can read with MAX. Use the manufacturer to help you through translation problems. There is usually someone who has solved these translation problems before. Users groups are also a good source for this type of information. Never overlook the option to write your own translation program. Sometimes you get from "A" to "B" by way of "C."

CHAPTER 7 PREPARATION

THE MECHANICAL DEVICE

Situation: You will be working with an existing model that was created by the machine shop of a manufacturing company. The prototype, because of the revisions made during the creation of the parts, looks quite beat up. You have been asked to produce a still image or computer-generated illustration to show what the final product will look like for sales promotion purposes. You are also being asked to animate the assembly procedure and produce an animation that will portray the functional operation of the product.

Given: You will have access to a physical, operational prototype from which to take measurements and study the operation of the product. You will not be allowed to remove it from the place of business.

The virtual model will be created from your measurements of the physical prototype provided by the manufacturer. Either they did not build it to drawings or there may have been corrections made between the release of the drawings and the machine shop assembling the final part.

The animated assembly will serve two purposes: an assembly tool for manufacturing personnel and part of the advertising of the product by sales personnel. A functional animation means that they want to study the motion of the parts involved and they want to have you make it "operate" in the animation.

BEGINNING THE MODEL

MODELING DECISIONS

There are many ways to approach this problem. My choice is to sketch the product on paper and build the model directly in MAX. If the drawings were available or I were asked to draw the engineering documents, I might have made different choices.

Advertising has provided you with color chips and a sample of the metal to be used on the model. Since you are working from a model rather than drawings, it is important that you take precise measurements the first time and that you get all the required measurements at the first meeting. Asking for opportunities to remeasure makes you look unprofessional, though that is preferable to making a mistake in the model.

HARDWARE RESOURCES

Some considerations that must be a part of your estimation process will be based on time. How long do you have to collect information? How long do you have to build the model, set it up, render it, review it, put it to tape and add music? Time-based decision-making means that you must always be mindful of the deadline at each point in the process.

Another consideration you have is a series of options to buy or make what you need. You can hire a courier to take your samples to the local service bureau to have them scanned while you sit at your computer and model; or you can hire someone to model while you shoot live background footage. You can choose to model parts in clay and send them out to be scanned rather than attempt to hand model them in the computer (an option often chosen by character animators). Each of these decisions must be based on getting to the completion date on time vs. your profit.

You must also look at what hardware you need to have, or which pieces you need to rent. Scanners and light boxes are standard tools of the trade yet many people choose not to get them right away. Video output devices, including large storage devices, are often purchased at a later date.

MATERIALS

Your best resource for materials is a 35mm camera and observation. Great rust material samples can be shot from trash dumpsters. New construction sites have spangled metal surfaces and fresh weld textures.

LIGHTING CONSIDERATIONS

The wooden handles of the drill—both the main and the crank handle—are to be fire engine red, glossy enamel. All metal parts (except the gear teeth) are a medium blue. Gear teeth are a 70 percent gray matte finish after heat treatment. The gear teeth have no paint, as this would interfere with the operation of the gears.

CAMERA TECHNIQUES

Compound motions where both the camera and the parts move are undesirable in product illustrations. The camera will remain stationary and will use a 35mm lens.

SPECIAL EFFECTS, BY HAND VS. PLUG-INS

You can visualize the final animation, imagine the parts coming off screen and assembling, one at a time, like magic. Then the fully assembled drill gears begin to turn in harmony with one another. Imagine the highlight on the glossy red enamel rotating with the large red wooden handle. If we put a subtle lens flare, keyed on this pink highlight, it should make the product much more exotic.

OUTPUT

The output will be one 18" x 24" glossy Illustration, suitable for framing. Additionally we are to deliver a 5000 x 4000 x 24 bit .TGA format file on a ZIP cartridge: one-assembly animation, two minutes in length, no background or music, and one assembly animation with background and sound. The first is for manufacturing, the second for sales as a promotional tool.

FORMAT

The illustration is to be mounted on 3/16" foam-backed board, with a three mil. (.003" thick) plastic lamination. The two videos are to be delivered as 1-BETA-SP and one VHS each. The MAX file, all maps and all materials are to be returned to the manufacturer upon completion.

TIME TO COMPLETION

You have 30 days from the date of receipt of the down-payment to complete the animation. You retain the right to use copies of the piece for self-promotion and contest entry, but you must not show them for 90 days after delivery.

CHAPTER 8 CREATING THE PARTS

ANALYSIS

The analysis of the model should begin with an accurate hand sketch. Drawing both sides (and more views if necessary) is a good way to begin discovering the construction of each piece.

As you are drawing the piece you become aware of the shapes you will choose to rough in the parts that make up each of the bigger pieces, and how these pull together to make the assembly.

I choose to start with the most complex piece in an assembly. I find that when that is analyzed completely, the rest of the assembly is easier to understand.

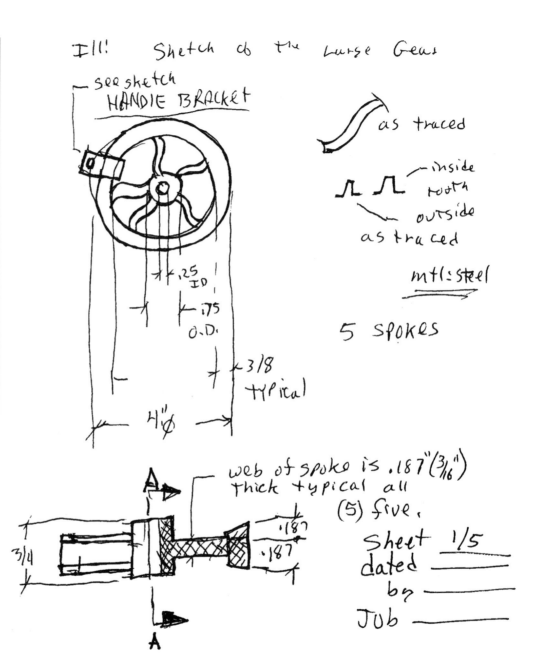

Ill! Sketch of the Large Gear

— see sketch HANDLE BRACKET

as traced

— inside tooth
— outside

as traced

mtl: steel

5 spokes

.25 ID
.75 O.D.
3/8 typical
4"ø

web of spoke is .187" (3/16") thick typical all (5) five.

.187
.187
3/4

Sheet 1/5
dated ———
by ———
Job ———

A
A

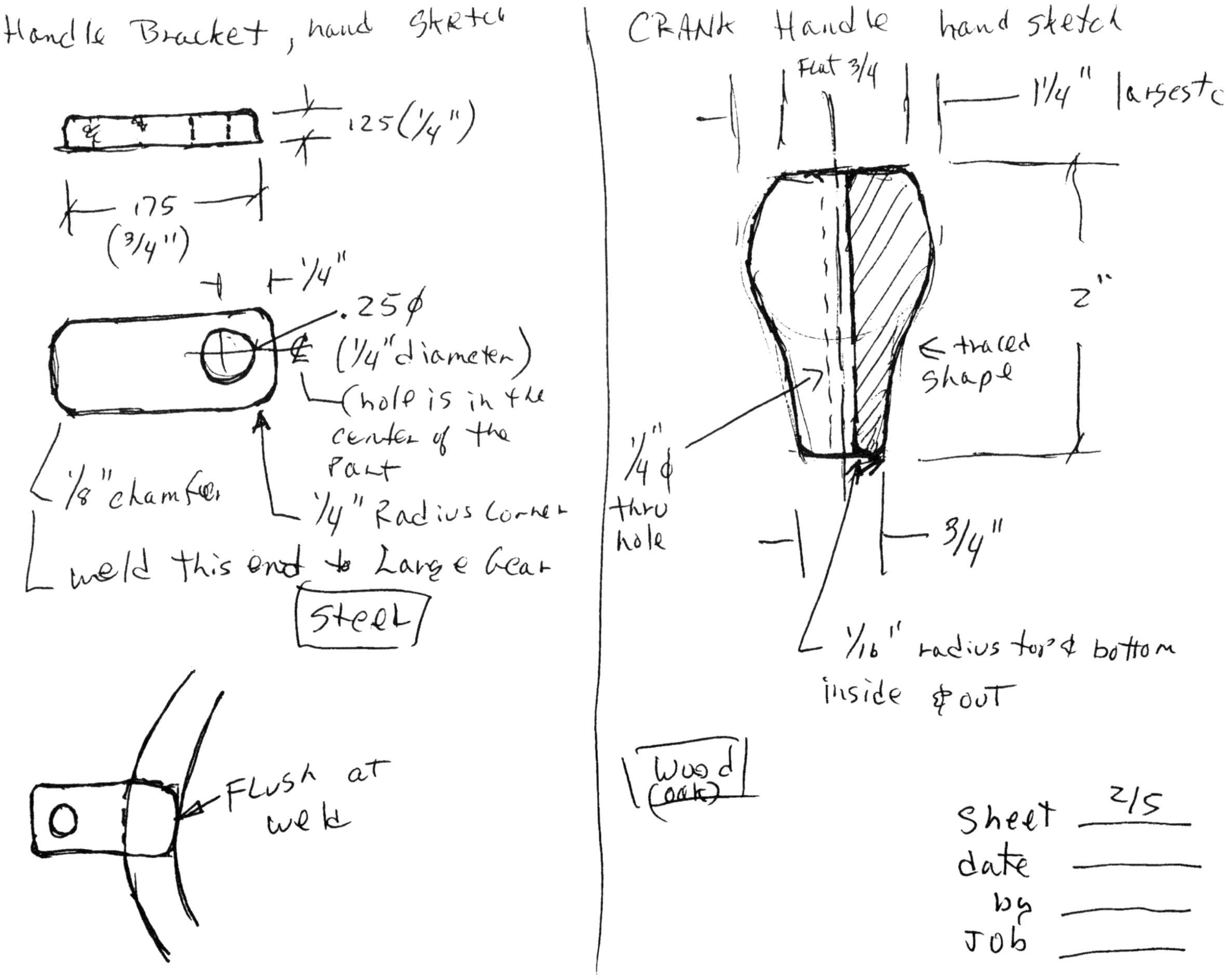

Handle Bracket, hand sketch

125 (1/4")

175
(3/4")

1/4"

.25⌀
(1/4" diameter)
(hole is in the center of the part)

1/4" Radius corner

1/8" chamfer

weld this end to Large Gear

Steel

Flush at web

CRANK Handle   hand sketch

Flat 3/4

1 1/4" largest ⌀

2"

← traced shape

1/4 ⌀
thru hole

3/4"

1/16" radius top & bottom inside & out

Wood (oak)

Sheet _____ 2/5
date _____
by _____
Job _____

SMALL GEAR/THREADED SHAFT ASSEMBLY

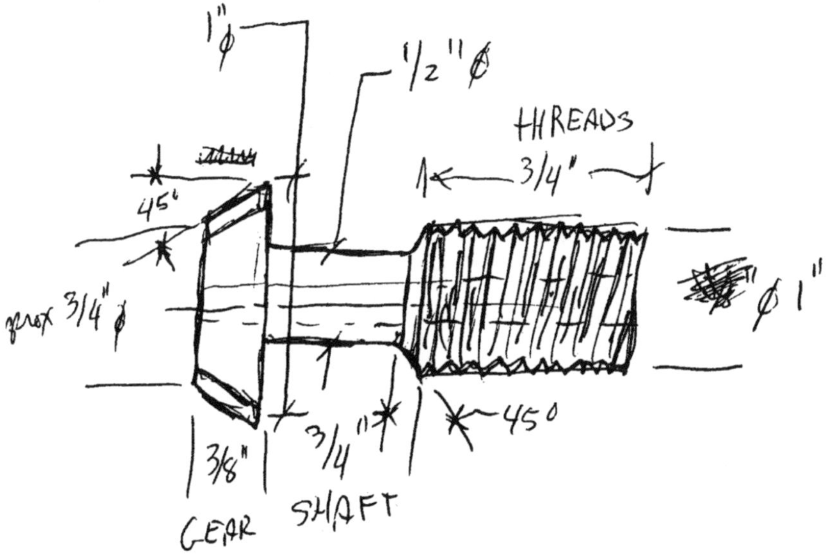

1" φ

1/2" φ

THREADS
3/4"

45°

prox 3/4" φ

3/8"

3/4"

GEAR   SHAFT

45°

φ 1"

JAW SEGMENTS
SPRINGS

.003 φ wire

5 turns

3/8"

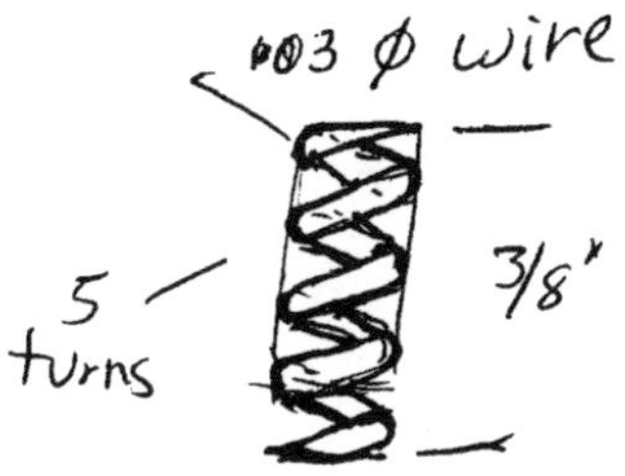

make 3
Black (Hardened) steel

Jaw Segments

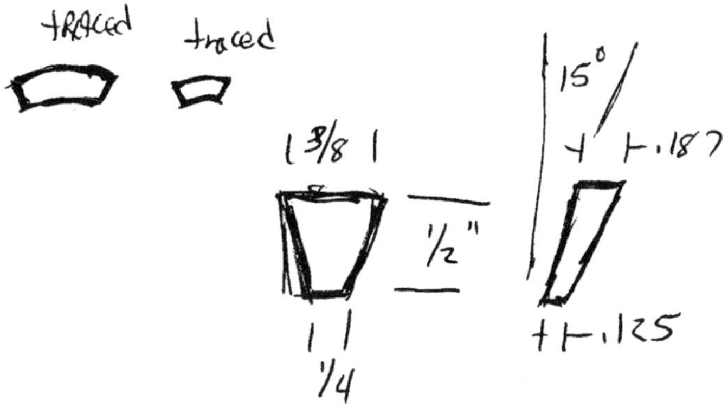

tRAced   traced

3/8

1/2"

1/4

15°

.187

.125

Sheet _____ 3/5 _____
date _____
by _____
job _____

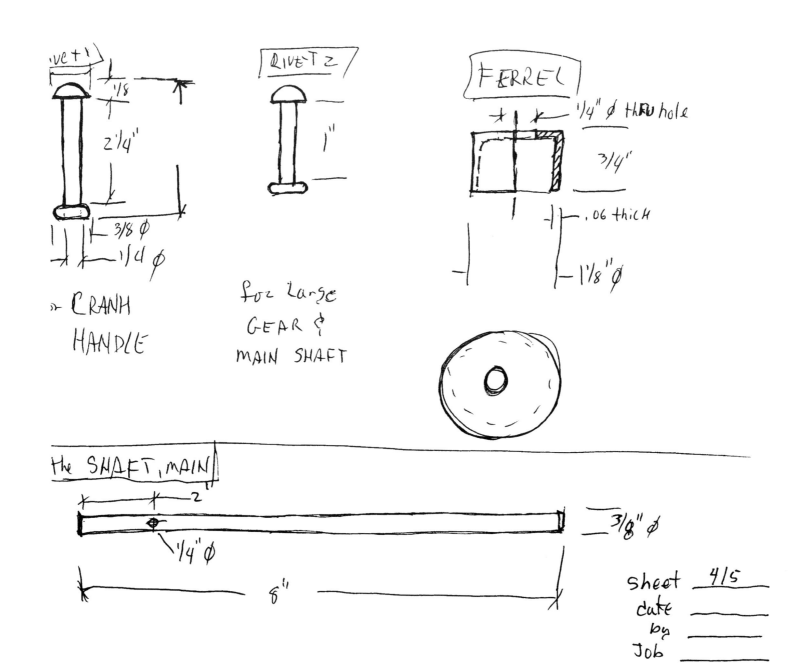

RIVET 1

'18

2'14"

3/8 ⌀

1|4 ⌀

» CRANH
HANDLE

RIVET 2

1"

for Large
GEAR &
MAIN SHAFT

FERREL

1/4" ⌀ thru hole

3/4"

.06 thick

1'8" ⌀

the SHAFT, MAIN

2'

1/4" ⌀

3/8" ⌀

8"

sheet ___4/5___
date _____
by _____
Job _____

TRACING

It is probably best, as with the curves of the spokes in the big gear and the end views of the teeth of the gear, to trace a profile of the handle on paper. Do your calculations and fill in the dimensions with the part and tracing in hand.

Don't hurry. The sketches and measuring, done correctly, should take one to two and a half hours depending on your skill. Imagine that you are making the part, not just measuring it. Ask yourself, "What dimensions do I need to create this piece?"

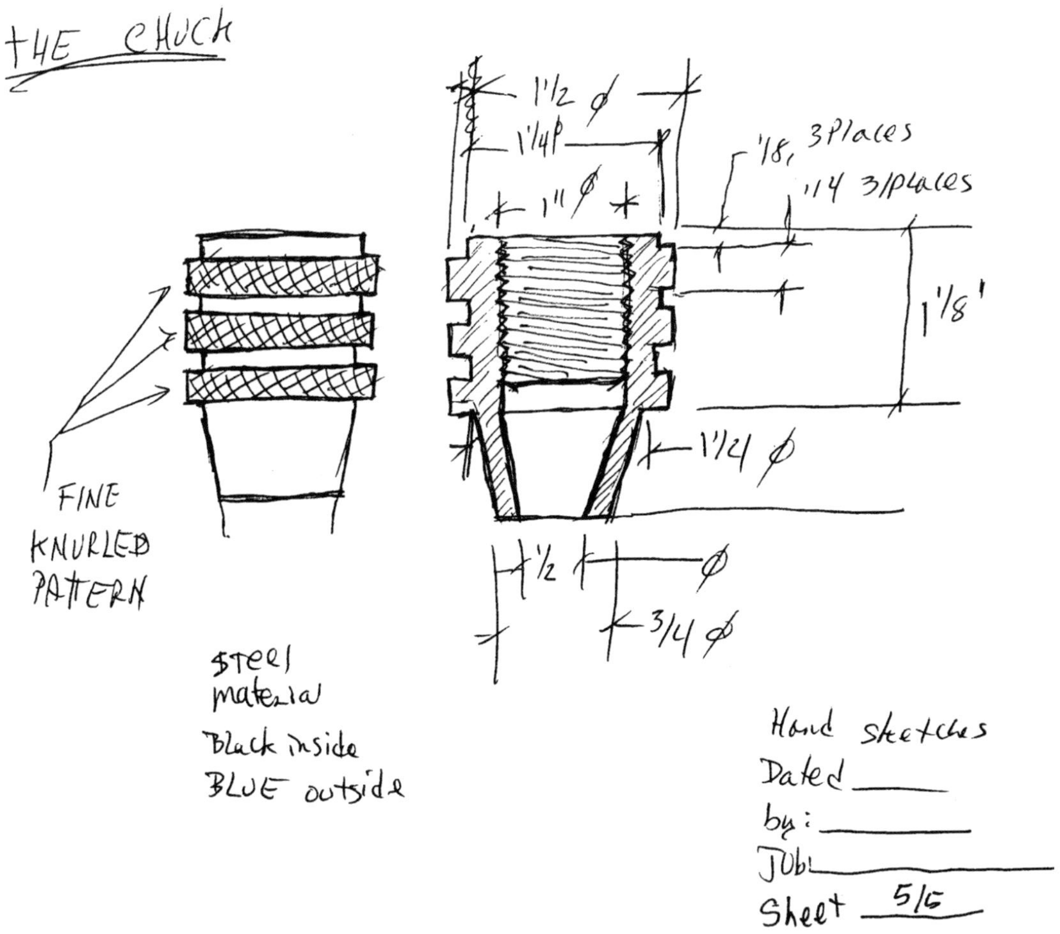

THE CHUCK

FINE
KNURLED
PATTERN

1'½ ∅
1'¼ ∅
1'' ∅

'/8, 3 Places
'/4 3/places

1'/8'

1'/4 ∅

1'/2 ∅

3/4 ∅

STEEL
material
Black inside
BLUE outside

Hand sketches
Dated _____
by: _____
JOb _____
Sheet ___5/5___

THE LARGE GEAR

If you can think of the hubs in terms of their primitive equivalents in MAX, you will see that they are both TUBE entities. In order to reproduce them in MAX, you will need an inside diameter, an outside diameter, and a thickness. Any additional features–such as rounded corners, keyways, or cross holes with set screws–would require additional annotation and sketches. Be sure to double-check seemingly obvious features such as number of spokes and the orientation (relationship of these other features to each other) of the details.

Create both the spokes and gear teeth from cross sections lofted along a path then array the results. For the spokes it would be a good idea to trace the shape while the model is in hand. Guestimating the curvature later is not a reliable method. Take accurate measurements of the thickness and width and sketch the cross section. Check the thickness and width at each end and the center to be sure it is symmetrical.

The teeth can also be traced with a sharp pencil with the outer shape set on a piece of paper. Do the same for the inside. The teeth aren't the same profile inside as out: In fact, they taper. Measure the length of the tooth: This will be the length of your loft path. Array the lofts and put the pieces together.

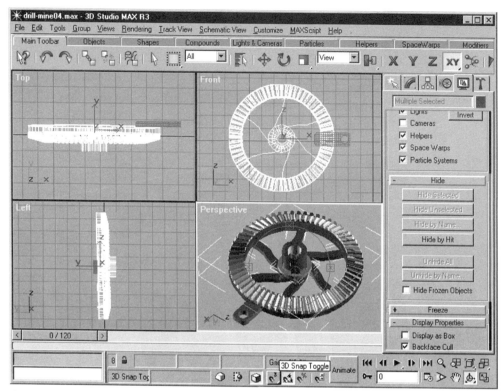

The large gear shown is made of four simple shapes: the inner hub, the outer hub, the spokes and the teeth.

HANDLE BRACKET

This piece of metal stock, welded to the gear after it is cast, connects the large gear to the crank handle shaft (essentially a thick rivet). It is a deceptively simple piece.

Several approaches to creating this part can be imagined. Start with a 2D rectangle and loft using fit/deform and define the profiles for the rounded edge in one direction and the chamfered corners in another; then Boolean out the hole. This solution is time consuming.

Another possible solution is to start with a box and punch out the hole. Then create three "tools" to subtract the filleted and rounded corners from the box. This solution will prove to be unstable (probably crash).

A simpler solution, though less elegant than the first and not as sophisticated as the second (though much more direct and faster), is to create the part with thirty segments along the length, ten in width and ten in depth. By selecting and moving the appropriate vertex or groupings of them, it is possible to simply slide these control elements into place to create the fillets and chamfers in minutes. Then subtract the hole and your part will be very stable.

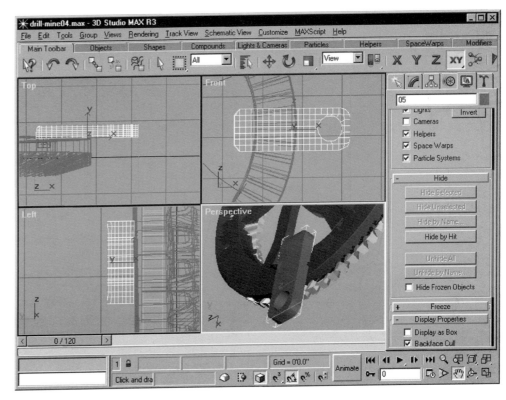

Some parts appear deceptively simple, but are not.

CRANK HANDLE

The handle can be analyzed in terms of its symmetry. It is a cross section revolved around a central axis.

In your mind's eye you must imagine that this piece has been cut in half vertically. The surfaces that show on the cut face form the cross section. Shaped like a letter "P," its axis sits just left of the vertical line that makes up the left side of the "P."

With this in mind, you need to know the overall height, the smallest and largest width of the whole part (half that measurement, minus the central hole, will give you the size of the cross section) and the diameter of the central hole.

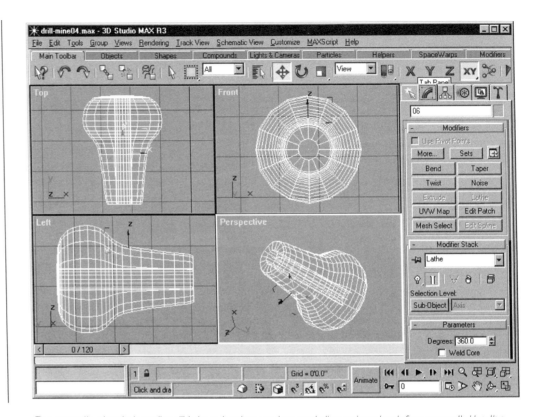

The smooth, simple handle will take a tracing and several dimensions to define correctly. Use the ruler tool to help you scale it to size. Scan your tracing/sketch and bring it into the background to use as a template for drawing the profile line. Be certain that the image is set to scale to the file, not the screen, or you will introduce distortion.

HANDLE PROFILE

The profile is created using the line tool (spline). The more time you spend with this tool, the more confident you will become in the creation of organic shapes.

You can use the ruler tool to check the accuracy of your profile at as many points as you measured from the original.

The ruler tool can be a great help with many measurement problems. It is one of the most neglected tools in the MAX tool box.

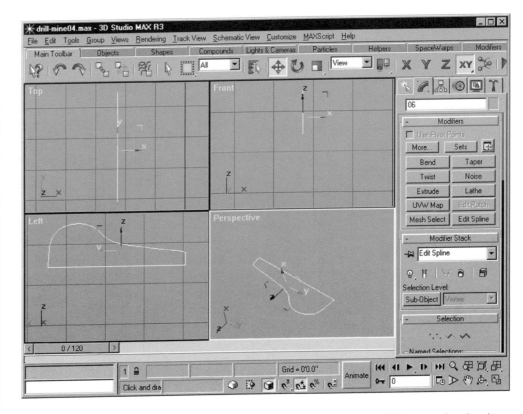

The spline curve is the basic tool of choice for any organic shape that exhibits symmetry about an axis.

THE RIVET

The rivet can be done by either of two methods. One is to revolve it about an axis like the handle; the other is to create a primitive and move the vertices.

Choosing the second method, the best basic shape to begin with is the shape closest to the final shape desired. I chose the capsule from the extended primitives list and set twelve height segments along the long axis.

Select modify/edit mesh and subobject/vertex. By selecting the center ten segments and using the scale/uniform modifier, you can have the capsule take on the second shape illustrated. Without changing the selection set, switch to the move tool and select the Y direction filter. Move the selected vertices vertically until the underside of the rivet head looks like the third example.

Select the lower few rows of central segments and move down to form the lower ridge with theY filter still on. Select and uniformly scale down the upper head until the final shape is achieved.

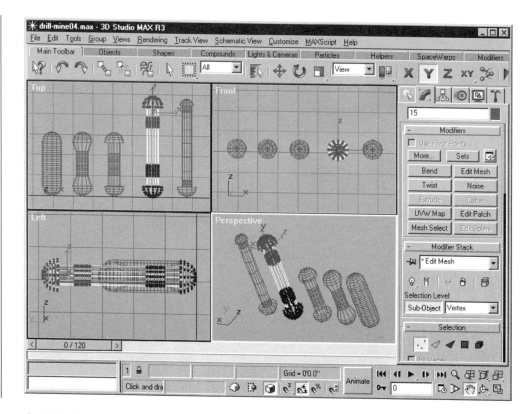

Sculpting by scaling and moving is a much more stable process than performing Boolean operations, and does not require the skills that drawing with spline curves can demand. Be sure you lock in the appropriate axis when using this method to eliminate distortion.

THE FERRULE

The ferrule was created by using the lathe modifier with a simple "L" shape spline curve about the default axis. The beveled edge was part of the original spline.

If it becomes necessary to modify the size or shape of the spline or to relocate the axis in order to change the size of the inner hole at a later date, it is easy to go back into the stack, or history of the part, and select and change these elements later.

To change the inner hole size, select the object; then under modify/subobject, choose the axis. It can be moved with the move tool.

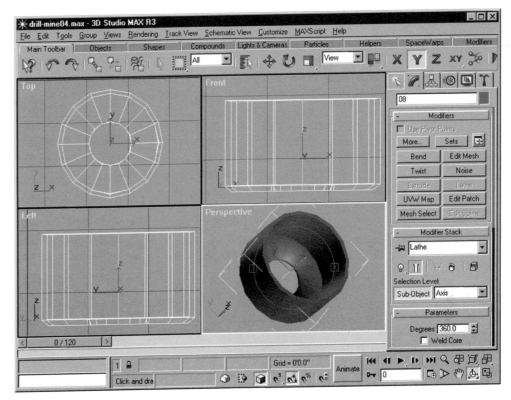

The ferrule is a spun or stamped sheet metal cover used to keep the drilled end of the wooden handle from splitting open. It is a thin cross section and MAX (and many other 3D modeling programs) sometimes have trouble representing these. If you see holes or tearing in the surface, increase the number of lateral surfaces or segments.

THE SHAFT

The central shaft holds the other parts together. It is a simple cylinder primitive that was modified by punching a hole for the large gear rivet by using a Boolean/subtract.

The Boolean2 operators in r3.0 of MAX are more stable than the 2.0 version. Notice the error in the top view. Extra faces were created on one end of the hole.

If the animation were to show a close-up shot of this area, hand-editing to correct the unnecessary faces would be necessary.

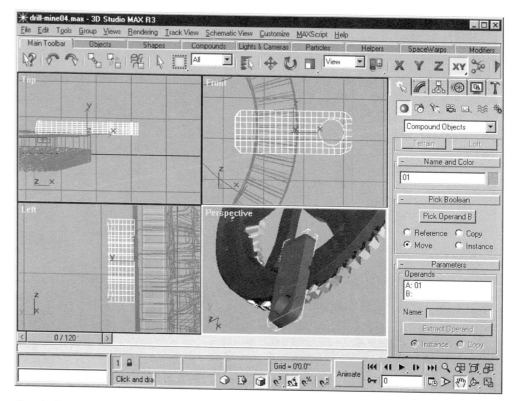

The shaft was created using two cylinder primitives. The second (smaller) cylinder primitive was set at 90° to a first (longer and larger diameter) tube and a Boolean/subtract operation was used to punch the cross-hole. Note the extra faces left in error across the end of the hole.

SMALL GEAR AND THREADED SHAFT ASSEMBLY

The gear has been combined with a threaded end piece intended to accept the cap of the chuck. The parts have been combined for simplicity of handling later during the animation phase.

The gear is drawn and documented the same way as its larger counterpart. The body and threaded head are added by combining different length and diameter cylinder primitives.

The first tooth was created using a loft from the small end to the larger one. It was then hand edited at both ends, at the vertex level, before the array was created.

The threads are not modeled for two reasons. The first is that the file size would increase significantly. The second is that they will only be seen in motion and a map of the threads with bump added will create the illusion of threads until the chuck cap slips or spins over the end.

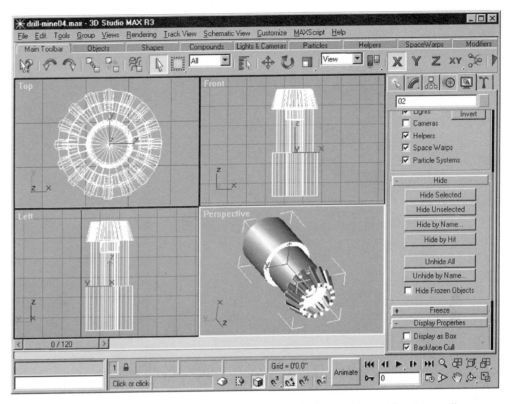

When multiple parts will translate or rotate together it is easier for you to combine them with a group command in advance.

JAW SEGMENTS AND SPRINGS

The three segments of the jaws are created with a simple loft from a smaller profile to a larger one. The offset is accomplished by pulling the end vertices at a subobject level.

Array was used to get the three parts 120° apart. The springs are a circle lofted along a helix.

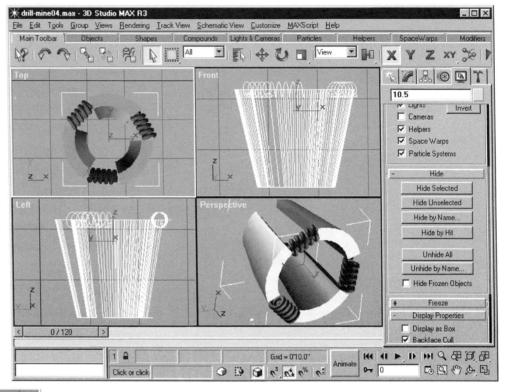

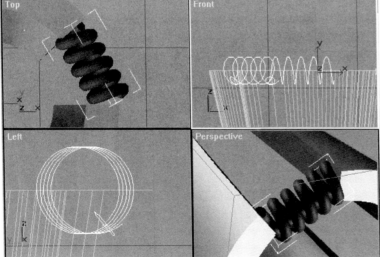

The springs are a simple five-turn helix with a small circle as the loft shape; array is then used to create three copies of the helix.

THE CHUCK

The chuck is a cylinder with about fourteen vertical segments. The segments were scaled and moved much the same way the capsule was turned into a rivet.

The parts intended to be tightened by hand will have a knurl; to model this would be impractical and drive the size of the file up too high. The same look can be achieved with a simple black and white bump map applied to only the knurled surfaces.

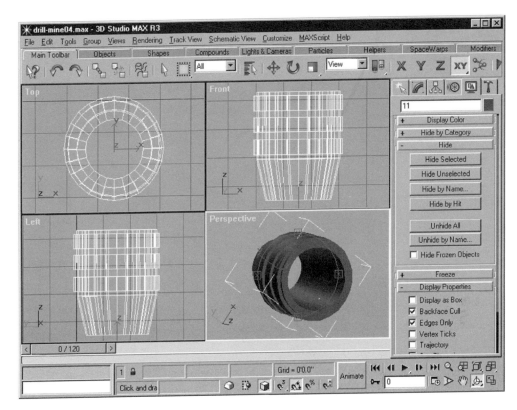

The chuck looks complex, but is really quite simple.

Use the circular selection set option. Change the ID of the whole object to ID 1. Then select the inner faces and invert the selection set to have only the outer faces that will be knurled later; selected, assign them material ID 2.

THE ASSEMBLY

Assembling the parts should be the easiest part of the job. If the parts have all been built correctly, they should easily slide into place.

I didn't have a perfect taper on either the chuck jaws or the inside angle of the chuck cap. After assembling the pieces, I grabbed the ends of the chuck jaws and scaled them slightly to make the angles match.

The need for absolute accuracy is relative to the use of the model. If I were creating this model for a technical study, I would have reported the discrepancy to the engineering department. This model is for animation and doesn't have to be absolutely perfect.

Notice the rotation icon in the perspective window. I am beginning to adjust the view of the assembly right from the start. Selecting the most revealing angle is important to the client; showing the product to best advantage is your job as an illustrator.

The parts were created in separate sessions of MAX and saved under different names. Each is being brought into the assembly file separately. The file/merge option is used to add another MAX or older Studio file to a MAX file.

Sometimes the source is from an older version of 3D Studio. When the file extension is.3DS, you use the IMPORT option rather than MERGE.

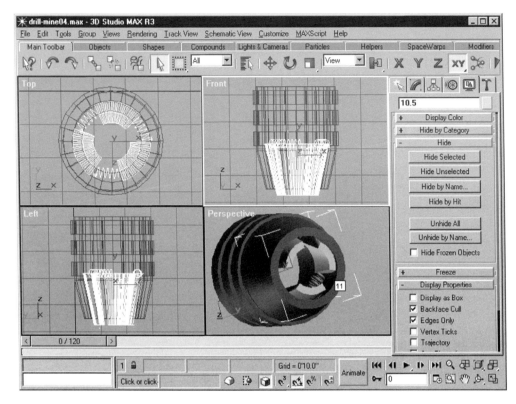

Assembling the pieces is the easy part, as long as they have all been built to scale.

CHAPTER 9 CREATING THE ANIMATION FOR THE MECHANICAL DEVICE

PREPARING FOR THE ANIMATION

All the parts are in place. In order to animate the gears turning together, the large gear (which consists of two tube primitives) many loose teeth, the spokes, the handle bracket, the crank knob and the crank knob rivet must be collected under a group name.

Once these pieces are selected and grouped, it becomes evident that the axis of revolution of the assembly is off center. A new axis point must be chosen that is in the center of the inner hub.

To accomplish this translation of the axis, the parts must be grouped; then the axis can be reset as shown here in stages.

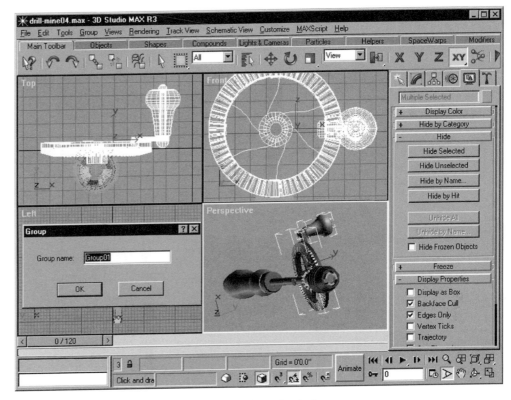

Parts of the assembly must be grouped in order to animate them.

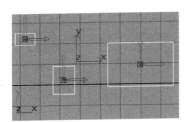

Three loose objects

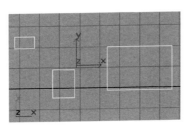

selected and grouped, new axis

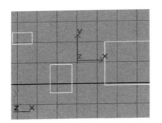

affect pivot only selected

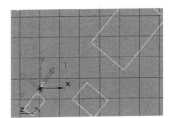

rotated about new pivot

67

THE FINISHED ASSEMBLY

Without the embellishments of materials, creative lighting, camera perspective or background, you now have the assembly in its simplest form. This is a good time to check the model against your notes.

Check the fits of the parts in wireframe mode. Do the inside diameter of the gear hub and the rivet body line up perfectly? Does the knob and the bracket on the gear match the height of the rivet or is the rivet head sunk into the wood? Correct any errors you find before proceeding (if you jump ahead of the checking step and have to revise the model after applying maps, The mapped materials may distort and the mapping icons may have to be removed and replaced to get a good image again).

After you check the model, it is time to begin creating the materials for the various parts of the assembly. Use the color samples or Pantone paint colors you were given by the advertising department. Multi-subobject materials will be required for the threads on two of the parts. Creation and application of this material type is well defined in the MAX tutorials.

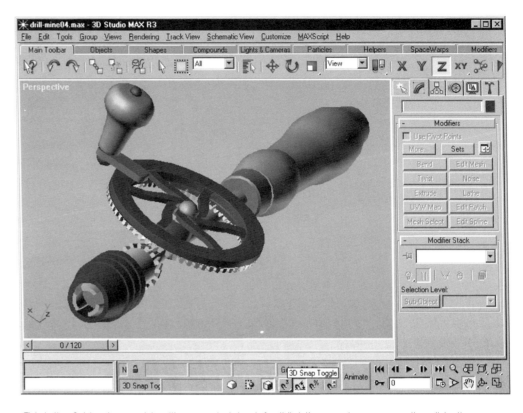

This is the finished assembly with no materials, default lighting, and no perspective distortion (caused by the camera). This is the ideal opportunity to review the model for accuracy before the beautification begins.

ANIMATING THE ASSEMBLY

I began by numbering the pieces in the order in which I wanted them to appear in the assembly as a technique to make the process less confusing.

You may also give each of the pieces a name. If you choose meaningful names at the sketching stage, try to keep these names throughout. In a simple assembly such as this, the use of numbers and names helps to keep things that way. In the case of an assembly with hundreds or thousands of parts, it becomes impossible to function at the animation stage without a naming convention that you have stuck to throughout.

You may need to name groups and subgroups as well as parts in your naming or numbering structure. Without any structure you will soon become hopelessly confused and frustrated. In order to animate smoothly later, you must spend the time on the names up front. This becomes even more important if you are working with someone else, or teaming on a large project.

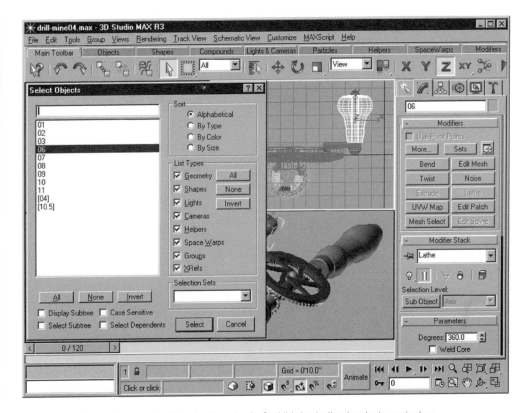

Naming each part properly will make it easier to find it later in the track view window.

TRACK VIEW

The track view may seem like an esoteric representation of the movements of parts in an animation, but it is very user friendly and can save hours of hand manipulation if you become familiar with its operation.

Numbering and/or naming the parts makes it easy to keep track of them and to see the orderin which they are to move in the track view window.

By manipulating the key frame dots, you control the relationship of the parts. By overlapping their start times and end position times, you can create overlapping movements in the assembly. Careful handling of this technique will make the animation more interesting.

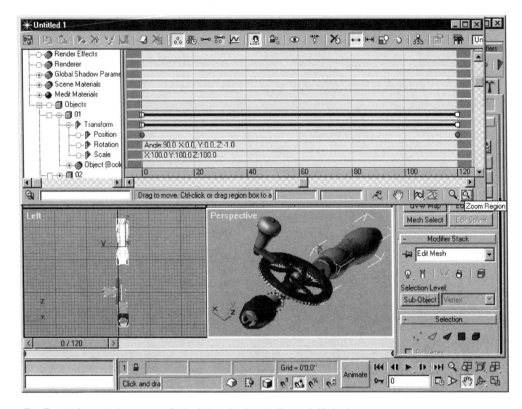

The Track View window, powerful but threatening to the uninitiated.

This is how the Logo would appear if placed over a starfield background with multiple flare effects in the background. Stronger shadows could have been used, but the color and value composition is clean as is.

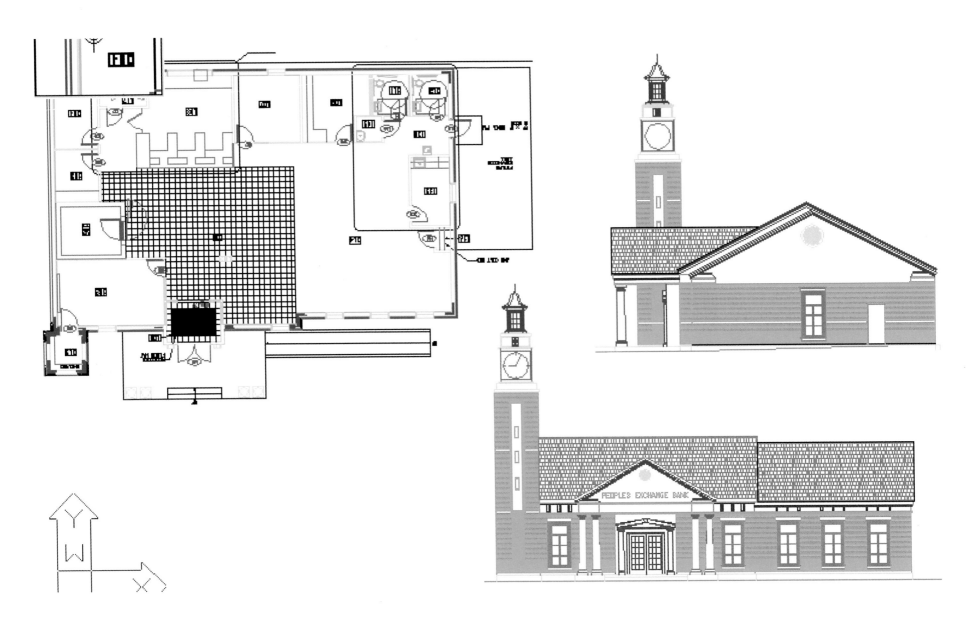

The AutoCAD 2D drawing is in need of some work before it is ready to serve our purpose as the basis of a 3D model. A great deal of removal of unneeded line art must be done.

The final image is rendered with three lights, from a camera height of 5'-6". The trees and the shadows they cast make an otherwise dull image come to life.

The hand drill special effects may be a little 1940s-science fiction overdone. Produced as a handout to support a corporate or engineering presentation, it would be an effective and memorable piece.

LET THE ANIMATION BEGIN

Press the play button. The parts begin moving into position from their off-screen locations. By keeping the track view window open, adjustments in the rate and timing can be made interactively.

Release 3.0 of MAX shows keys in the time slider to make it easier to see where the key frames are.

After each successful change in the animation, save your work. Assign different file names occasionally. Errors can creep into the animation (sometimes software-introduced, sometimes operator-introduced) and will make things move in unpredictable ways that are hard to trace. It is best to have a version to fall back on. Test frequently to confirm the effects of the changes you are making.

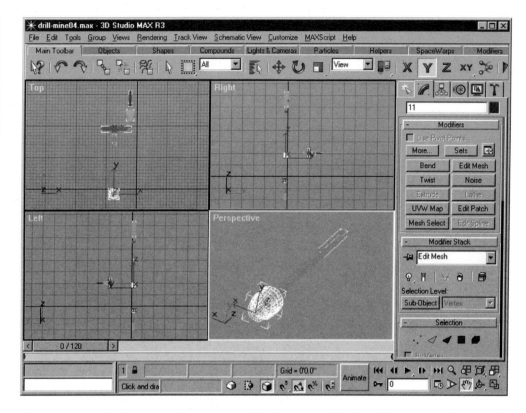

Parts shown moving into place from off screen into the perspective view. This can be replaced with a camera view later.

TIMING

The location of the key frames in the track view window controls the location of the parts over time. To make the pieces come into view in a specific order their start and ending locations at various points in time can be controlled by manipulating the key frames.

To slow something down, move the start and end frames farther apart over time. To speed it up, move them closer.

When acceleration and deceleration are involved, the TCB (tension, continuity and bias) controllers must be used to edit the starting and ending frame keys directly.

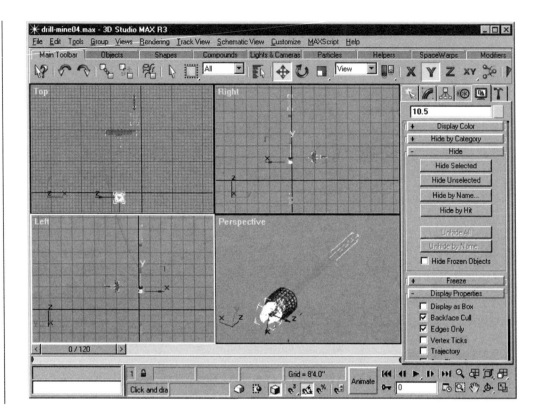

The order of the assembly is not always obvious in more complex assemblies. Consult with manufacturing personnel, as well as the designer, to get it right. When pieces have to pass through one another to get into place, something is wrong.

DOPE SHEET

A dope sheet is a standard form used by 2D animators to predetermine the number of frames needed to portray each action. The track view window serves this purpose in MAX. The alternative is to lay out the action on paper with a timeline.

Thinking through the order in which each piece should move from start to finish and jotting it down on a freehand chart makes it easier to understand how the assembly will work. With such a chart in hand, it is easier to manipulate the parts by name (or in this case, number) in the track view window.

Timing is important in assembly work, the operator has to have time between parts to physically get the next part. This is often accomplished by pausing the videotape player. You can accommodate this procedure by adding heads and tails to each operation.

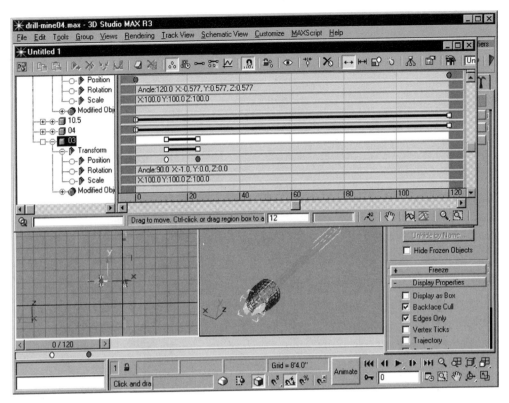

The parts will be assembled in numerical order. This way they can be read directly off the track view window. The parts are all starting to move at the same time. This will be corrected later. Note that the new markers in the key frame space under the scrub bar (r3.0 and r3.1) can be moved directly.

The standard dope sheet used in 2D animation can be applied to 3D as well.

SEQUENCING

The process of determining when each piece will enter the field of view is one of keeping a part in place until it is its time to move; moving it into place at the proper rate of speed; stopping it in precisely the right place; then holding it in place while the other parts come in and find their locations.

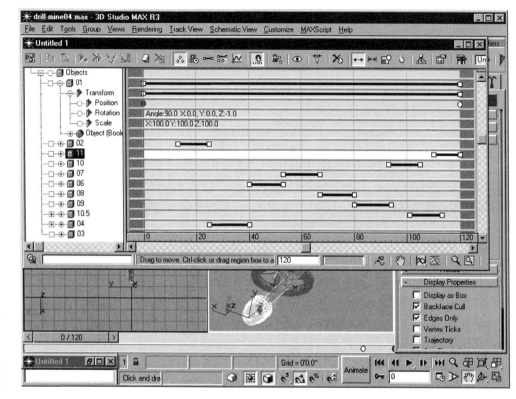

By arranging your screen to allow both the Track View window and the assembly to show at the same time, you can watch the effects of changes in the track view as they affect the animation in real time.

ADDING ADDITIONAL FRAMES

If the animation happens too fast, there are two ways to slow it down. To figure out how to have the parts take—let's say—45 seconds to come into place, we need to do some calculations. Forty-five seconds at 30 frames per second is 1,350 frames. We now have 120 frames. To increase the number of frames and to tell the computer to stretch the sequence we have so nicely arranged, we use scale time.

The second way to extend the animation time is as follows. The next sequence will need more frames—another 1,350 frames—to show the crank and gears turning nice and slowly. We must add frames to the end of the existing sequence without disturbing the first 1,350 we just stretched. This is done by increasing the total length of the animation without using scale time. Both operations take place in the time configuration window, but have totally different effects.

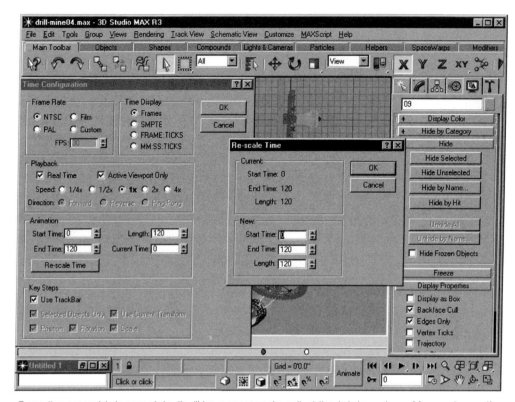

Once the assembly is complete, it will be necessary to adjust the total number of frames to see if the timing is correct. The total number of frames can also be increased buy adding copies of the last frame of the assembly to the end.

EXPRESSIONS

Expressions are used to set sequences that may not be possible to accomplish by hand. These are motions that require constantly changing calculations based on relationships.

Consult the MAX tutorials for a detailed explanation of the process.

This simple assembly can be animated by simply counting the number of turns each gear must turn and setting the rotation mechanically over time. Set the start and end key frames at 1,350 and 2,700 in this example.

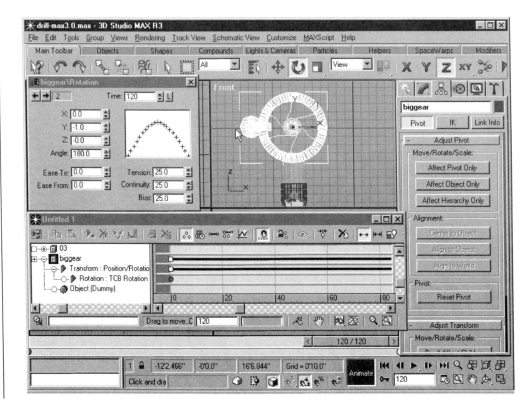

In a simple assembly you can set the rotation by hand.

DELIVERY OF THE ANIMATION

Most engineering houses have VHS players; few have Beta. Since your work may become part of a broader presentation at a later date it is a good idea to work on Beta-SP and keep the original in that format, but deliver the client a VHS tape.

Study the style and methods of hand-painted and air-brushed technical illustrations to learn what is customary in this market.

Initially, you may use your model to produce a still image or illustration for an engineer. This model may be quite simple, even dull. The same model may be reused to produce an animation for presentation to an entrepreneur or CEO. This will require more finish, color, and textures. The model may again be called upon for a slide presentation or animation for sales. The sales presentation piece may have special considerations to accommodate text and may require the creation of an additional flying-logo piece as an introduction.

REVIEW

In order to work with mechanical engineering drawings, you will have to learn some of their terminology. References to other drawings are made in the form of cryptic abbreviations, bills of materials (that can require some translation), and certainly help from the documentation person in the firm that produced the documents.

Most engineering drawings are detailed in two-place, three-place, and occasionally four-place decimal dimensions. Review your high school notes if you don't remember how to translate decimal and fractional dimensions.

Blueprints are inexpensive and usually disposable. Never accept an original document as reference. Original engineering documents are drawn or plotted on velum or acetate and are very valuable. Blueprints are usually clear enough for you to read and work from.

If you plan to work in this market begin now to collect fraction-to-decimal and metric conversion charts, thread size and hardware style descriptions and pictures, assembly tool dimensions, and material descriptions with pictures. You can build a library of common materials such as plastics and metals quite quickly with a flat bed scanner next to your computer.

JOB 3 THE ARCHITECTURAL FLY-AROUND

The architectural fly-around is a staple of many small animation businesses. Architects have always valued visual aids for the presentation of their concepts to clients. They also value visual aids as a method of working through their ideas before construction. Pen and ink and watercolor have been the hand-drawn visualization media of choice for centuries. 3D models give the client an approximate view of the final product. Computer illustration and animation are tools that can show the client an accurate picture of the finished facility without breaking ground.

Architectural illustration and animation can constitute a large market in any growing community. Computer illustrations range in price from $500 to $3,000, animations from $2,500 to $50,000. Although this is a quiet portion of the animation market, as opposed to Hollywood's special effects, it is well worth investigating as an income source.

Much of the work comes to the animator in AutoCAD format, 2D drawings or 3D models that can be passed to MAX. For many 2D to 3D conversion operations, it is faster and easier to work in AutoCAD until the model is at least partially complete, then pass the file to MAX to finish the modeling.

Many, but not all, animators learn AutoCAD because of its precision and ease in handling geometry. AutoCAD's primary limitation as a modeling package becomes apparent as models become more organic. AutoCAD is not a good organic modeler; there is no sub-object level to work with. AutoCAD objects are not parametric.

One of AutoCAD's strong points is its ability to handle Boolean functions. If you have a complex molded or formed plastic part that requires multiple subtract and fillet operations, MAX will not handle this well. I have used AutoCAD for as many as 100 consecutive Boolean operations without an error.

I have referenced AutoCAD throughout most of the following exercise and have created an appendix (C) at the end, noting the most useful AutoCAD commands for building models intended for eventual transfer to MAX.

THE PROBLEM

Object: Create a computer-generated image of a bank to be built in Kentucky. The image is to be used to sell the concept and later to be presented to the president of the bank when the building is completed.

Specifications: Plan and elevations (4) are provided in AutoCAD, r13 format. Final image to have, in additional to the building and immediate grounds, people, cars, and trees. Millwork details are provided.

Environment: Details are provided in the form of photographs of the site. The lighting is to be daytime, 10:00 AM to midday.

Working conditions: In 30 days the client needs a 36" × 24" photographic quality image, mounted on foam core, under glass, framed, with standard picture-hanging hardware included, in a crate ready to ship to the client.

Future work potential: Exists for an animated fly-around of the building.

Materials: Cement base is an unusual composite, 1/2" thick sample provided. A brick sample is provided. A sample is provided of the mortar for the brick, which is a special mix grey. A roof material photo (gray slate) is also provided.

Chapter 10 Making the Sale to Architects

Working with Architects

If you aren't familiar with the methods used by architects to represent information in graphical form, spend an afternoon or an evening or two in your local library looking at books of architectural drawings and illustrations. The documentation methods used by architects and the terminology they use is unique to their profession. You will not be expected to understand it all, but if you can't read the blueprint well enough to recognize the major elements, you won't instill confidence in your client.

The architect's needs for illustrations are very specific, and fall into two categories. The first are impressionistic illustrations that give the client the look and feel of a total environment. These are quick, painterly images, usually done with watercolor, marker and color pencil, or gouache. If you find that your storyboards have this look to them, you may want to tackle this type of work. If not, then you probably want to leave it to fine artists. The second are exact illustrations used for final approval or for those clients who can't visualize at all.

Many architectural firms have told me about a recurring problem they have had with watercolorists. Watercolorists are artists; they believe it is their job to make the architect's concept look good. They produce beautiful pictures regardless of the subject. The watercolorist's work is presented to the client by the architect and the client falls in love with the painting. After the building is completed the client and the architect stand on the street corner in front of the building to review the work. The client holds the watercolor in his left hand and with his right he points to the building and says, "This is a very pretty picture but it doesn't look like what you built me."

Architects tell me that they need an illustration that represents exactly what the building will look like, with no embellishments.

The architectural client who needs animation is usually a sophisticated buyer with a high-end client. The animation is intended to impress rather than educate. Accuracy is very important of course, but the look of the piece is more so. The polish on the entranceway brass lamps, the sense of grandeur and visual richness upon entering the front doors, the parking lot full of cars are details that become very important at review time.

Most architectural firms use AutoCAD for their working drawings. AutoCAD is a drafting and design tool that can be learned fairly easily. I am not going to attempt to teach AutoCAD here, but it is to your financial advantage to learn it as soon as possible. I have been a party to races between building architectural models in 3D Studio vs. AutoCAD on similar machines, and AutoCAD has always been the winner, sometimes by as much as 2:1. All the techniques I outline in AutoCAD have parallels using LINE and SPLINE editing, with EXTRUDE or LOFT and REVOLVE commands in 3D Studio MAX, but I find them much slower to use. MAX wasn't designed to do this type of work any more than AutoCAD was designed to create 3D mesh characters for animation.

The 3D functions of AutoCAD, or another CAD package capable of 3D modeling, can be used to complement the weaker points of MAX (such as its Boolean math operations). By learning a few basic AutoCAD commands such as bpoly, pedit, extrude, revolve, subtract, union, and intersection, it is possible to create a 3D model quickly from the 2D data.

Many 3D objects can be drawn and modeled most easily in AutoCAD; some are best done in 3D Studio; some others in Rhino,

Softimage, or by using MetaBalls. Making correct judgements in the selection of software before starting can prevent false starts and a lot of aggravation later.

The more geometric an object, the more easily it can be drawn in programs such as AutoCAD. Complex geometric shapes such as injection molded plastic parts with many curvilinear features and rounded edges and inside fillets cannot be created efficiently in 3D Studio without an undue amount of work. If you have an object with a high level of complexity that can be created quickly using multiple applications of geometric shapes and you are unfamiliar with AutoCAD, it may be to your advantage to subcontract construction of the model.

When the project calls for objects to be created in freehand proportions, or the shapes are basic geometry as opposed to complex, or if the organic forms are random or fractal (such as ocean waves or desert sands), and particularly when these shapes are to be animated, 3D Studio is the best choice. Most shapes created outside of 3D Studio are not going to animate or morph as well as those created in MAX. Shapes that are totally organic, such as characters, animals, and plant-like structures, can be created more easily using MetaReyes, MetaBalls, Softimage or Rhino.

In the case of the bank building, the people, cars, trees, and steeple are better candidates for 3D Studio than AutoCAD. Most of the rest of the file is distinctly geometric in nature, and therefore prime AutoCAD material.

Documentation from the Beginning

You will receive drawings and often samples from the architect from the first meeting. You should begin your work with a new client by creating a major subdirectory on your hard drive and appropriate subdirectories (suggestions to follow). Place a copy of their CAD drawing in one of those subdirectories and return their disks with their material samples (after scanning them; more on this later).

What to Expect

Architects create working drawings. They also create material sample boards or notebooks containing samples of the carpet, wallpaper, ceiling tile, cabinet door finishes, countertop material, marble for the entranceway floor, etc. They will give you these things along with the drawings and, often, bills of material. It is appropriate for you to ask for interpretation of their documentation methods. They may be totally proprietary, so you are not expected to understand how all the pieces relate or how to connect, say, each of the three ceiling tile samples with the areas they are intended to go onto. As with the logo project, you cannot ask enough questions or take enough notes.

The first thing you want to do with the samples is take them to a scanner. Capture high-resolution images of the items and return the items, the next day if possible. These must be handled with utmost care. The sample set is usually the only one that has been created for the job; a great deal of time went into collecting the materials and their presentation. If you scan the brick and stone samples on your own or a service bureau scanner, be careful that you don't scratch the scanner glass. It is a good idea to use a thin sheet of clear, rigid plastic to put between the gritty item and the scanner top.

Reviewing CAD Drawings from the Architect

Most AutoCAD and other CAD operators have no clue as to what a 3D-model builder needs to create illustrations and animations. When I am offered drawings, I politely tell the client, "I need to look them over to see how they were created," before agreeing that they may be a source of valuable information. Their method of creation may or may not speed up the process of illustration or animation. They may become a consideration in calculating the price. Some badly done CAD drawings are more trouble than help.

To check a CAD drawing for the degree of modeling knowledge of the creator of the file, check the following items first:

1. Look closely at corners to see if they are closed. Corners that don't meet indicate that you have drawings created by someone who guessed at locations. The shapes will take you a great deal of additional time to rework into a form that can be extruded into 3D objects without costly and time-consuming manipulations.

2. Select random dimensions and attempt to move them to see if they are intact. If the pieces (such as text, leader lines, etc.) move individually, then they have been exploded (or the dimaso variable was turned off during their creation), and none of them are reliable. If this condition exists, then you will have to check the dimension shown against the actual size of each item.

3. Randomly test, particularly long lines, outside walls, etc., to be sure that they are continuous. Erase them and regenerate the image to see if there are segments that were coincident or if stacking segments end to end has been used to create the line. Either of these practices, though they may not affect the usefulness to the drawing in 2D, will create problems later when you attempt to create closed polylines for extrusion into 3D shapes.

4. Take a serious look at their layering conventions. If the groupings are logical, i.e, if there are layers that are specifically

separating outer walls, windows, doors, plumbing, etc., good. When a layer, say the one with only windows, is the only one turned on and you see some plumbing fixtures and a couple of office plants on that layer too, the drawing is not going to be efficient to work with. A related problem is discovered when you turn off all but one layer and find things on that layer that are not the colors of that layer. This means that the operator used the over-ride feature on color; and it is impossible to export the drawing to 3D Studio MAX using the by-color option without a lot of time-consuming cleanup.

FIVE METHODS: THE MODEL FROM AutoCAD TO MAX

1. Export from AutoCAD by layer to .3DS format
2. Export from Autocad by color to .3DS format
3. Export from AutoCAD by object to .3DS format
4. Using the .DXF or Drawing eXchange Format
5. Import into MAX directly as a .DWG format

Each method has advantages and disadvantages. Using the EXPORT from AutoCAD as a .3DS file format with the by-LAYER option selected creates a series of objects where every object on a layer is linked into a single object under an object name that is the name from the AutoCAD layer. All items on layer glass, as an example, become a single object called glass when it enters 3D Studio MAX. If all the glass in the model is blue, this becomes a good thing. If the panes of glass all face the same direction and you want them to reflect the scene that they are facing or be mapped with a common scene from behind the camera, then this is ideal. However, if glass is on two perpendicular planes and you wish to map each plane separately, the segments will have to be separated later. It is better in this case to create at least two layers, one facing direction A and one facing direction B, name the layers GLASSA and GLASSB and separate them.

The second option, export by color, allows each thing that is (for example) green to become a single object regardless of its layer. If you find a drawing where everything is drawn on a single layer, say layer zero but all walls are green and windows are blue, this could work for you. Simply export it as is and work with it as long as there is no wallpaper with patterns on the walls or reflections on the windows.

The third option, export by object, is used when every object in the AutoCAD file is to be imported into MAX with a different name. This applies when the entire AutoCAD file is on one layer but the entire AutoCAD file has been built of reliable POLYMESH solids. This option creates many objects in MAX and takes a very long time to import.

The pros and cons of method 4, using the .DXF file, are documented in the next chapter.

Method 5 is new and not well documented; my experience with it so far has been excellent.

TIME-BASED DECISION MAKING

In every job involving a 3D model, there is a make, subcontract, or buy decision to be made. When the items are totally custom, like the building in this case, they must be built from scratch in 3D. You can opt to build them yourself or hire a subcontractor to build them for you. In most cases you will use your skills to build them yourself.

In some cases, a model may be too complex for one person to build in the time available or your knowledge of that field may be limited. You might need to pay someone to help you interpret the prints. Another reason for subcontracting is that you may be too busy to build the model portion of the project yourself, feel you can complete the other steps yourself at a later date, and don't want to lose the job.

There are also people, cars, and trees in this package. You may find that some perfectly acceptable people can be had from the many Web sites available that offer prebuilt models. You may not, however, find the type of cars you need on the free sites and may choose to buy models from one of the many businesses that stockpile models of all types and will sell rights to you at a reasonable price.

Another source might exist for the cupola on the top of the bank tower. Many manufacturers now offer, either from their own Web site or on disk, models of their products that can be had for free or for a nominal price. In this case I did various Internet-based sorts and finally called the manufacturer of the cupola in question. Although they did not offer such a library, always check: It is a good investment in time and you can expand your own library.

CHAPTER 11 BUILDING THE MODEL

SCANNING AND TRACING

The materials provided to you in this case were brick, cement, a mortar color swatch, a paint swatch and a photo of the type of roof slate used. Each of these can be handled fairly simply, but deserve some explanation.

If there is a way to use the simple color generators in MAX, this is the material that will render most quickly. If the material can be created using one of the procedural maps, that will render the next most quickly. If the material contains maps, with or without other modifiers, these materials take the longest to render. The choice of whether to use a scan of a material sample provided as a map or as reference should be based on this. The best material is the one that will give you the most faithful rendition of the material in the shortest rendering time.

The brick could not be created with its mortar pattern by any simple means in the material editor. It was therefore a prime candidate to become a scanned material. The brick should be scanned on a flat bed scanner, which requires you to lay the brick on the glass of the scanner. The brick may contain granules that are harder than the glass bed and scratch the surface. Keep a sheet of thin Plexiglas in your work area (if you own your own scanner) or in your trunk if you use a local service bureau for scanning. This is true of all objects you are given to scan: ceiling tile, marble samples, wood, etc. Once the scan is created, it must be taken into PhotoShop and copied as many times as necessary to create a repeatable or tileable pattern. The mortar color must be placed in appropriate bands between the brick pictures to create a full illusion of brick with joints.

The photo of the roof material may or may not be useful, depending on the manner in which it was taken. If the picture was shot from the ground it is only useful as reference, so you can try to match the look. If the picture was shot with the camera perpendicular to the roof surface, then it may be useful as a map to be used directly on your model.

The samples of the paint could be scanned but that would not yield the most efficient material on your model. A more efficient solution would be to match the color in a Pantone or similar color swatch book and then create that color in CMYK[1] using Adobe PhotoShop or Corel Photo Paint and converting that color to its RGB equivalent to view on screen.

[1] CMYK is an abbreviation for Cyan, Magenta, Yellow, and Black. This is a standard color system used to define inks or paints to create a uniform standard for colors. Each Pantone color swatch has a name and or a number assigned to it and a CMYK value that can be used to recreate the color precisely. RGB stands for Red, Green, and Blue. The RGB color system was created to describe colors produced by mixing colored lights to create new colors. The RGB color system is used to describe the colors produced by a light source, such as by a television or computer monitor.

TAKING OUT THE TRASH

Drawings created by the architect always contain more information than you need, assuming that your goal is to create a model to be used for an illustration to be done from a predetermined point of view. Let us say that the final image is to be viewed from the front right, eye-level, viewer standing approximately 50 feet back, in the parking lot or street out front. From this point of view, the rear and left ends of the building, the inside and any features (sidewalk, parking lot, trees, etc.) would not be seen and need not be modeled.

Dimensions are useless, as are features which refer to section details. These can be erased. Bills of material and blocks containing both graphical and alphanumeric data can be exploded to extract the graphical elements and the data portion erased. Once the unnecessary stuff has been removed, the business of building a 3D model can begin.

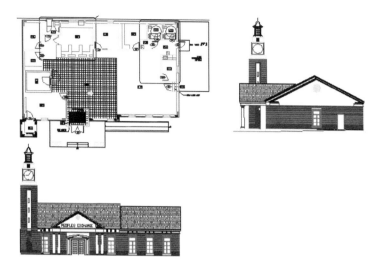

AutoCAD drawing, as received: three views, one plan, two elevations.

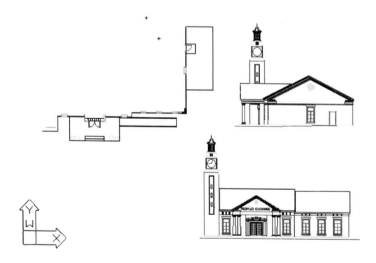

AutoCAD drawing cleaned up in AutoCAD and brought into MAX. Unnecessary lines, textures, and text are removed. The rear and far left walls of the building will not be seen and are also removed.

FILE STRUCTURE

Save your modified file and create a subdirectory structure on your hard drive to use for this client or project exclusively. Keep your original AutoCAD files in a separate directory. Keep your current working file, both 2D and 3D, in separate directories as well. Your scanned materials as scanned and the manipulated versions need to be separated. Text files such as running notes, copies of the original proposals and bids, contracts, etc., also deserve their own subdirectories.

STUDY THE ELEVATIONS

Elevation drawings give different information about the building than the plan and can be used slightly more directly. The leftmost element shown here is the front pillar. If you refer to the plan view, you can see that there are four of these. By zeroing in on that area you can extract a half-section profile to be revolved later in AutoCAD or by using the LATHE function in 3D Studio (depending on where your experience is greater).

The height and width of the window casings, sill, header, and mullions (dividing pieces that create the rectangular patterns with the glass) can be extracted from this view. The door information, diameter of the round vent, angle of the roof (pitch), and end view of the fascia are defined in these views as well. The most direct piece of information that can be extracted from these views is possibly the height of the main walls and of the overall structure of the tower.

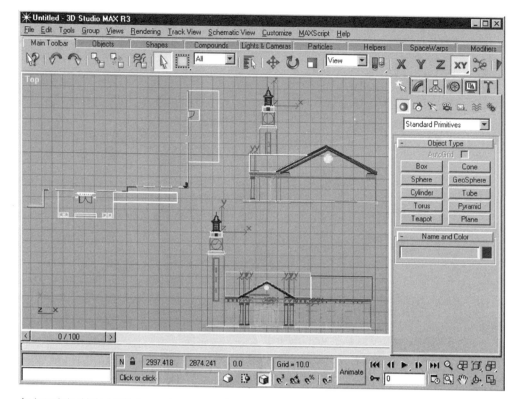

As translated into MAX, three views, one plan, two elevations. This is much smaller than the original file.

DETAILS OF THE ENTRANCEWAY

Only in this view can we appreciate the detail in the front entranceway header, the shape of the entranceway doors, the section of the smaller pillars on each side of the front door, the smaller peak vent, text location and the details of the two size blocks in the fascia. Such details and dimensions must be observed and measured here.

The text is the Simplex font, native to AutoCAD. That should send up a red flag; ask the architect for a sample of the actual logo used by the client (in this case, People's Exchange Bank). A sample is preferable to simply asking the name of the typeface because there are variations of the typeface by name and it is too difficult to ask whose version of Arial was used. Frequently there is a variation of the typeface or even a single letter variation to make the logo distinctive and worthy of trademark.

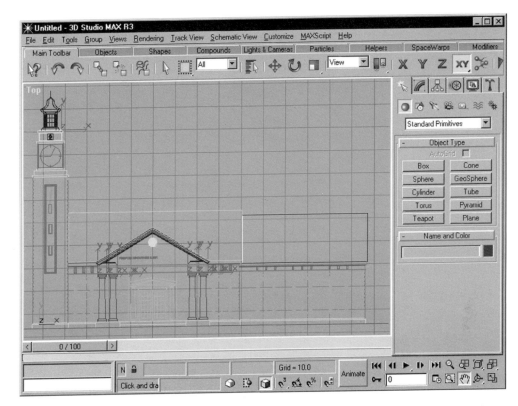

This is the front elevation of the bank. Notice that the text has become undersized in the translation to MAX.

SELECTING TYPEFACES

I use Corel Draw as a first resource when I am looking to match a typeface. The selection of 1,000 fonts provided at no additional cost has afforded me 100 percent matchup with most typefaces I have been asked to match and model over the past nine years. Corel has mastered spline curve controls for those occasions where a deviation to a standard character is called for, the kerning features are easy to use, and WYSIWYG.

The final manipulation can be converted to curves and exported as a .DXF directly into AutoCAD and extruded (and the holes in the letters subtracted) quickly. The 3D text can be exported as a .3DS format file and imported into MAX. Why should you go through this complex procedure? The number of fonts available through Corel Draw is unmatched, as is the ease with which you can manipulate every aspect of the text. If you have additional fonts from the architect or client, you can install them in windows and then access them using the create/splines/text function in MAX.

CONTROLLING MODEL SIZE

The Boolean functions in AutoCAD are superior to those in 3D Studio MAX. However, only in MAX can you control the number of faces generated on the curvilinear surfaces by using the parametric feature. When you want each letter to be a separate entity (such as when you want to place a different material on each letter), they can be exported by object and they will enter MAX as individual entities.

In this case, the customer has changed his mind. On a similar bank they noticed a concrete decorative structure consisting of 8" × 8″ squares alternated with 8″ × 16" rectangular pieces and would like this integrated into the design with brick, rather than the slag stone originally drawn. Samples and a hand sketch are provided to you to accommodate the modifications. You must make note of these changes so you will remember to bill your architect/client for the additional work.

In the long run this will make a smaller model.

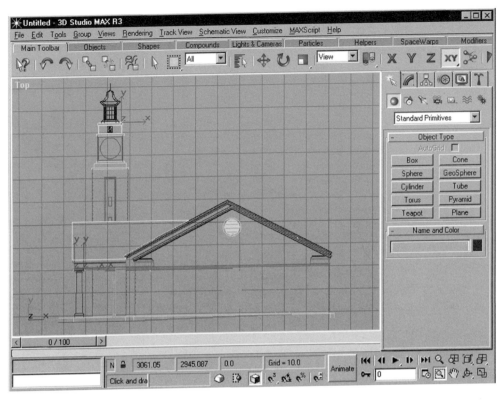

This shows the elevation view of the bank with the unnecessary detail removed. It is prepared for extrusion into 3D.

Planning Ahead

The easiest way to perfectly scale the brick (sample provided) to the front and right side wall segments will be to map each individually. Since the new corner blocks are 8" and a brick course with mortar is exactly 2", you will need to scale the brick exactly four courses of brick to each corner block.

Because of the addition of the decorative block, you must not allow the brick to become even slightly out of alignment; this would be very noticeable. To assign individual mapping icons to each wall face, each of the walls must be a separate entity. Seven separate segments will have to be prepared: one for the right wall (the holes for the window and doorway will be subtracted later), one for the front right, one for the small piece of wall that jogs toward you, and one for each side of the front door. It will also be necessary to create wall segments for the front and right side of the tower.

The brick needs only a flat wall. The change in design has significantly reduced the total geometry required. The brick scan can be used as a material map as well as forming its own bump map (when used in the material editor). This will create an effective 3D look on the brick walls and will require less geometry than the original design.

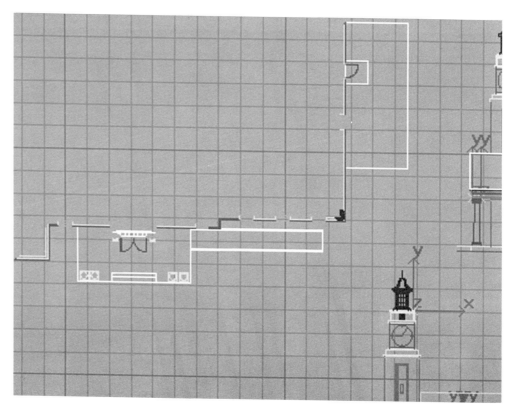

This is a plan view showing the relationships of the walls. The use of patches to replace the original walls will make for a much smaller file and allow individual mapping of each flat surface that needs brick.

NOTE: The walls can be made from patches. patches cannot be used to perform Booleans (in this case, to cut window holes out of the walls) but solid shapes, such as a box, can be used to cut holes in patches. Patches make small.

THE CONCRETE BASE

Working in MAX, it is time to create the concrete base, the entry steps, the single step outside the right side door, and the access ramp in the front. These can be constructed of simple box primitives. Create the ramp from a wedge, or create the ramp as a box and pull the upper two vertices on the right down to the ground or sidewalk level.

This may be desirable because the ground or sidewalk level is not known at this time. Tracing the appropriate profile and extruding will give you each of the remaining concrete parts very quickly.

NOTE: If at some later date the client should decide to have you produce a 360° walk-around or additional views from the other side or rear, it is essential that you keep all the original data for later reference. You may need to restore materials you deleted earlier, as well.

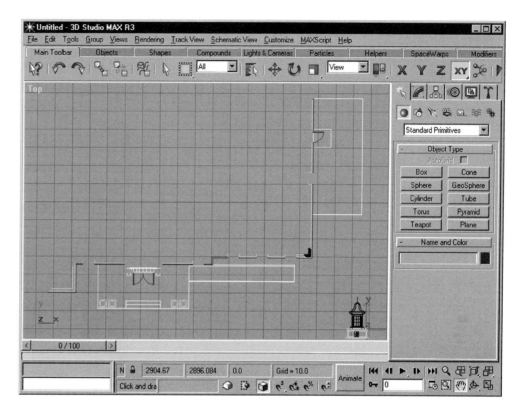

The concrete base has been brought back from the previous erasures in order to have an accurate base.

CUTTING OUT THE WINDOW HOLES

Create box entities for the door and window shapes and subtract these from the basic wall patches. Be sure you are viewing the pieces in several viewports so you can be certain the boxes are through the wall segment (or patch) before subtracting. The openings should be slightly larger than the visible window opening and smaller than the outside boundaries of the framework or sash.

Profile drawings of each of the moldings on the building should be available from the architect. These can often be used directly to create the basis for the extrusions that make up the trim on the model. Obtain these as early as possible and place them in their own subdirectory.

By using the bpoly command in AutoCAD you can create a polyline outline of the face of the peak in a single pick on the screen. Make your next command sequence extrude/last, then enter a minimum value such as 4". This way a large area of geometry is built very quickly. Use the dist command or look on other drawings to get an accurate cross section of the fascia moldings. Use these dimensions to create a closed pline shape. Use the dist command to get the length of these moldings. Extrude the pline profiles to these distances. By creating a pair of box entities you can subtract the excess material and create a perfect seam at the peaks and do the same at the bottom edges where the trim meets the front and rear fascia. The

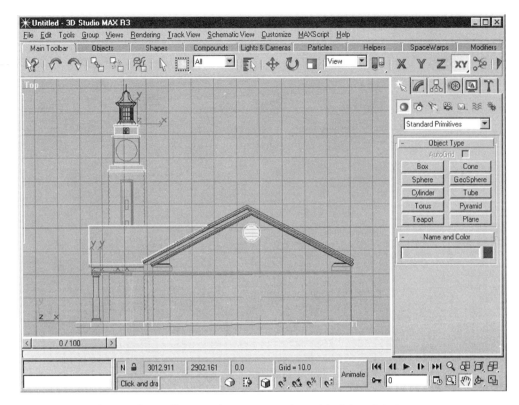

The peak triangles are stucco. They are, from a geometry point of view, flat planes.

returns can be created using the same extrude profile and subtract the excess method. The door casing, header, and sill follow much the same pattern. When you have created the pieces of the window, of course group and copy them for use in the front of the building.

The circular vent in the face of the peak area can be created with a tube extruded a couple of inches for the frame. Be certain to create a separate cylinder a couple of inches thick and recessed below the surface of the frame or a circle that will be flat mapped later. This additional circle of geometry will later receive a material consisting of nothing more than black and white stripes to create the illusion of louvers.

USE MAX OR AUTOCAD?

The roof and segmented overhang can be created more easily in MAX than in AutoCAD. The window casings and eight-sided base for this capitol can be made as three polygons, two for the eight-sided base elements and a third for the eight-sided window part. After extruding the base pieces a couple of inches each, the window portion is extruded to its four-foot height. Three box objects can be created, crossed 120° apart through the window extrusion and subtracted to create the window portion all at once. The glass and cross pieces are simple box shapes.

The flat area with the recess that holds the decorative, stylized trees (the logo of the bank) can be made as a box with two more boxes subtracted to create the recessed portion. More about the logo pieces later.

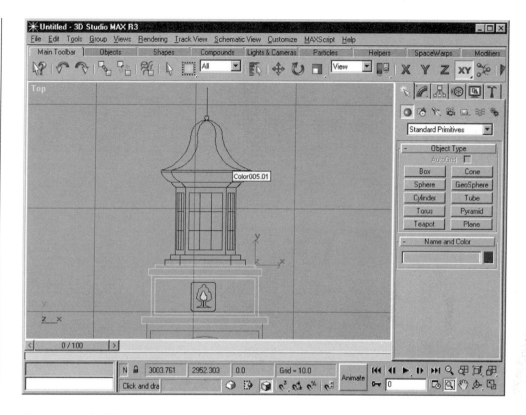

You can create this as many parts or only a few, depending on your ability to visualize the sections that must be extruded.

SMALL SECTIONS VS. BIG PIECES

Build the right side and face of the tower as trapezoids (as seen in plan view) and extrude them to the height of the top walls. You need only construct a box entity the height and width of the recess with a couple of inches of thickness and subtract to create a smooth recesss. If you used patches, you can subtract a box to create the hole and then add a box with one side removed tocreate the depression (you will of course have to invert the faces to see the inside, as the normal faces will be inverted). The decorative blocks are box objects. The frame molding around the edge of the recess can be created as one piece by drawing a rectangle and a closed spline profile of the molding and loft along the rectangular path. Repeat the procedure on the front.

Though it might be possible to do the entire tower as one profile extruded along a rectangular path, I have found that the resulting shape can become extremely unstable after the Boolean operations that must follow. It is my sugggestion that you do not do the brick portion of the tower as a single box but rather as separate pieces. Each outward facing surface must be planer mapped separately to get the brick proportioned correctly. MAX has a feature that allows you to get the map from one object and apply it to another at the same scale. That technique will work perfectly here. (Don't forget to make a copy for the side wall as well and rotate that copy.)

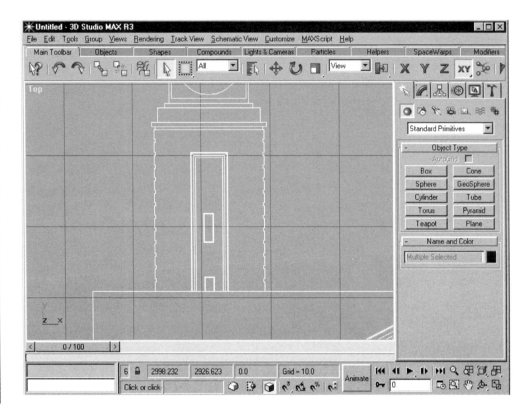

The tower has the geometry of the brick rows, it must also be mapped, and the two must be lined up with one another. The client change eliminates that problem, and creates another.

It is only necessary for the single illustration shot to create two of the four walls (those that will be seen from the camera position). In the event (not uncommon) that later you will create an animation using this same building, you can copy and rotate these same walls for the other two sides with little additional work.

For now, keep the geometry to the minimum. Always create as little geometry as possible, but never forget that you may have to finish the entire structure—or at least more of it—as conditions change.

LATHE THE COLUMN

The half-section of a column is all that is needed of the detail to make easy work of a complex piece of geometry. Draw a line from the midpoint of the topmost rounded portion of the column to the corresponding point on the base. Remember that the capitol (topmost part) andthe base (bottommost part) of a Doric column are boxes and should be made separately; they are not rounded top to bottom. Using both the vertical line and the outline of half the outer parts of the column as the trace boundaries, lathe the resulting closed spline.

AutoCAD users, revsurf (see more on revsurf and revolve later) the resulting pline about your midpoint vertical (axis), 360 degrees, and create blocks, using the box command, for the base and capital.

SPECIAL SITUATIONS

If you find that bpoly gives you an error, zoom in close and pan around the edges until you find an opening in the profile. If the opening does not become apparent through visual inspection, attempt to use the pedit, join option and select all the line segments that form the borders. Pressing enter after this operation should show the shape status by the first option toggle, i.e., if the pline option line's first word is "Close," then the shape is open and the command is offering to close the shape. If you select "c," you close the shape. When this happens, you will usually see a new line form connecting two seemingly unrelated points. This

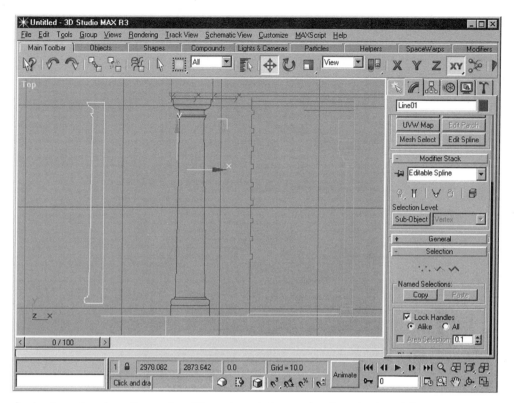

By drawing a line down the center of the column to be used as the axis of revolution, you can trace the column profile easily.

indicates that either one end of the line (or both) represent points to look at to find openings or overlapping lines in the group of lines you are trying to join. Another possible problem arises if two lines are on top of each other. AutoCAD joins them in such a way that they appear to be correct, but they will not extrude or revolve later in the process. The solution here is to change or create a new layer, make it current, and trace the shape with a new pline, and extrude or revolve the new shape.

MITERED CORNERS

The end view of the fascia trim can be used to extract the cross section for an extrude operation with very little work. You do not have to close the shape before you extrude it in order to be able to bevel later (using the Boolean subtract command).

The extrusion lengths can be measured from the front view on either side of the trim above the door. Use the Front Elevation of the Bank illustration and use the same procedure to extrude the remaining pieces of fascia.

To miter the corners of the pieces you have extruded, begin by building a box. The sides must be about two times the longest dimension of the profile of the extrusion you plan to miter.

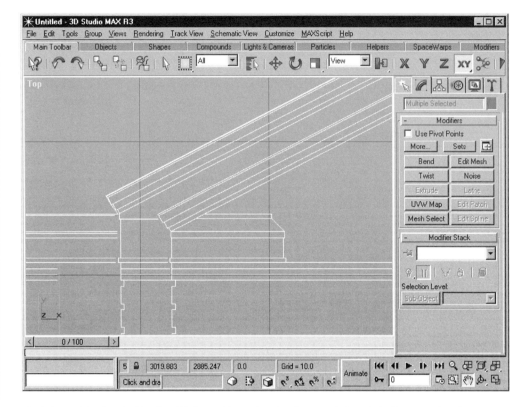

End view of the fascia. Use the 2D line art to determine the angle to rotate the extruded fascia (roof edge) after you create it.

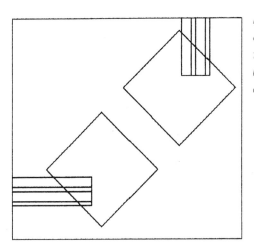

Rotate the box 45 degrees in either direction. Copy the box. Position the two boxes as shown.

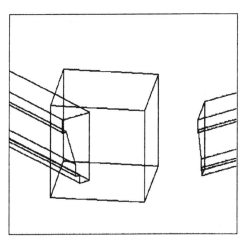

Two extrusions and the remaining box ready to be used to miter the other corner.

The mitered corner is complete. This process is necessary if the grain of the wood is to show. It is also preferable in models where the size of the building may change (as it often does with architectural projects). If the shape is common around a perimeter, then the loft (extrude in AutoCAD) can be done along a path that defines one edge of the perimeter. The miters form as the loft (or extrude) is created.

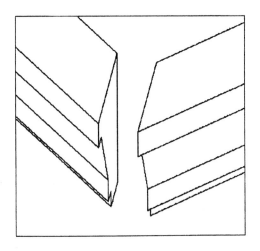

Select the right-hand extrusion. Use the subtract Boolean process and cut off the excess material. The left one is shown ready to process the same way.

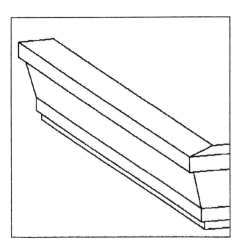

Both corners have been mitered and are ready to be moved together to form a joint.

To Model or to Map?

The same method used to create the fascia trim works well for the window casings (side pieces), header (piece along the top), sill (pieces that make up the bottom section), and mullions (the pieces that form the separations between the segments (lights) of glass) and the apron (piece below the sill). The cross segments of these pieces can usually be found on a detail sheet. If they are not provided, ask for them.

When creating a model strictly for animation–or where the camera will not pass closely to a detailed area–it is better, from a speed of rendering point of view, to make the window casing as a simple box and create a map consisting of a white field with gray vertical stripes to let a map suggest the geometry rather than building it. In the case of a still shot where the camera is fairly close to the model, you should build most, if not all, of the geometry to get the proper detail.

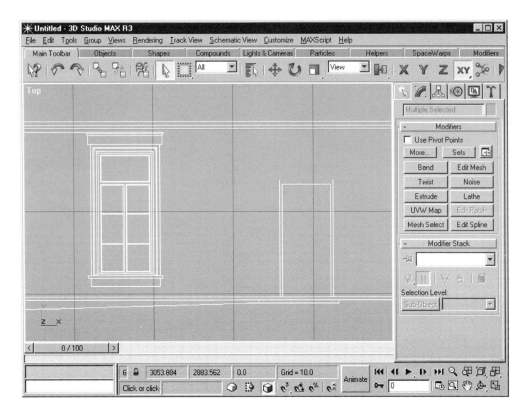

Check to see if the front windows are the same size and cross section as the one on the side, so that only one will have to be modeled. Notice the different widths of the various mullions.

The Roof and Other Angular Surfaces

To form the roof surfaces, use the spline command to trace the end view of the roof. Measure the length of each section from the plan view and extrude to those lengths. The illusion of slate material on the roof sections can be created using maps in MAX at a later time.

Extrude the roof edge trim horizontally and use the rotate tool to rotate it into place later; clip the corners as shown previously to form the peak joint.

NOTE: To trace something large (such as this peak surface) and maintain a reasonable level of precision using the spline command, it is necessary to zoom in close using the window option. (In AutoCAD, use the transparent or P and/or Z options, which allow you to pan and zoom in the middle of other commands without interrupting that command.)

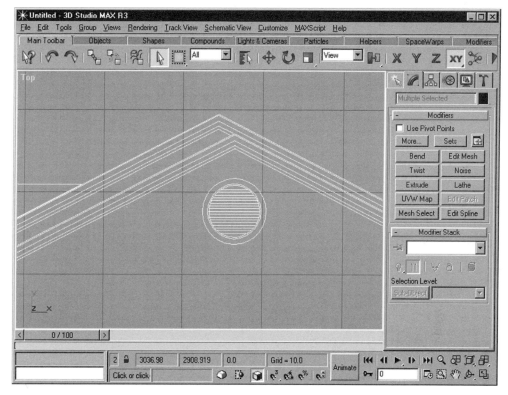

The roof surface can be formed by creating a simple rectangle to represent the slate. Extrude the rectangle to the full length of the building. The roof parts formed from the front of the entrance-way can intersect the longer pieces. The hips and valleys are unnecessary detail at this distance, but may be needed in closer shots and have to be formed later.

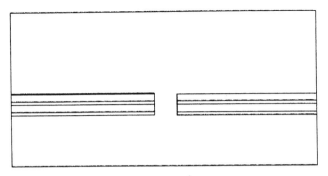

To form the roof peak, start with the extruded sections in plan view.

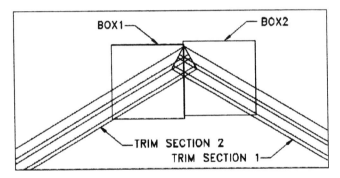

This is the setup, using the boxes in their original vertical orientation, ready to cut off the excess material from the roof fascia trim to form the peak. Using the Boolean subtract option, select trim section 1. Subtract box 1 from trim section 1.

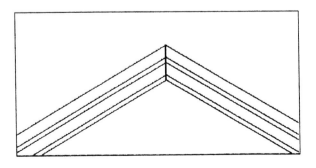

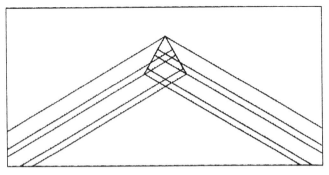

Rotate the sections to the proper angle and move them so that the topmost portions of the extrusions meet in a peak.

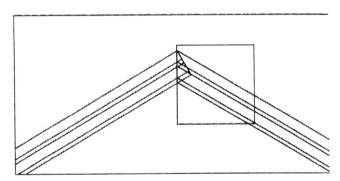

The right-hand subtraction is shown complete; repeat the process in reverse, selecting the trim on the left and subtract from it the remaining box.

The completed peak.

Note: It is actually better to leave a small (1/8" or so) gap between the segments. This gap will add a pencil-line wide seam to the junction and add realistic (an open seam) detail to the assembly.

THE PEAKS

The triangular face of the entranceway can be traced and extruded. Stucco will be added later to the front as a mapped material. Be sure that this area has its own triangle-shaped object and give it a name that you will recognize easily later. The horizontal member over the entranceway is one extrusion.

The returns, those pieces at the base of the triangle that turn back toward the main building, are made in two parts. The lower is an extrusion horizontally. The angled part on top is made from a rectangle that is drawn plan down from the roof and extruded using the bevel modifier later. Complete the sandwich with a box to form the top. Notice that there is an additional box that spans the tops of the pillars on either side.

It is easy to create the tapered portion in MAX by manipulating at the vertex level, rather than using the bevel modifier. Skip it for now.

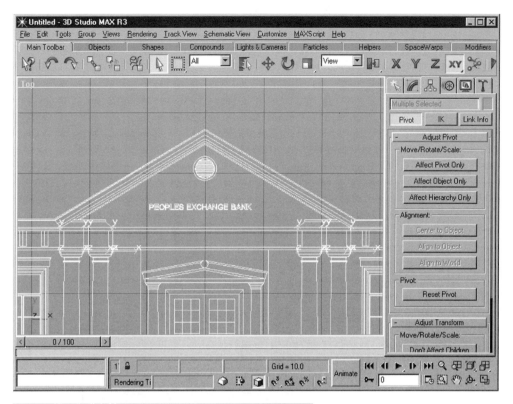

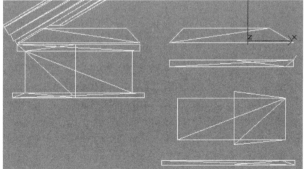

The front view represents a repeat of the procedures used to create the right view. The text can be treated as it was in the first part of the logo exercise in Job 1.

THE HALF COLUMN

The columns on either side of the door were formed using the same spline and lathe technique as the larger ones on the front of the porch, except that they were only rotated 180 degrees rather than the full 360. They could have been fully revolved and the excess left sticking into the wall; however, if at a later date the job were to expand to include a walk into the front door of the bank, you would then have to remove half the column or delete the full column and recreate the half column.

The doors are simple box objects with a hole subtracted out of the middle. The side window faces a different direction than the front. Copies of the side window must be rotated and the glass joined so the reflection is from a constant scene. If they were all joined, when the mapping was applied to the glass on the front, it would smear on the side window.

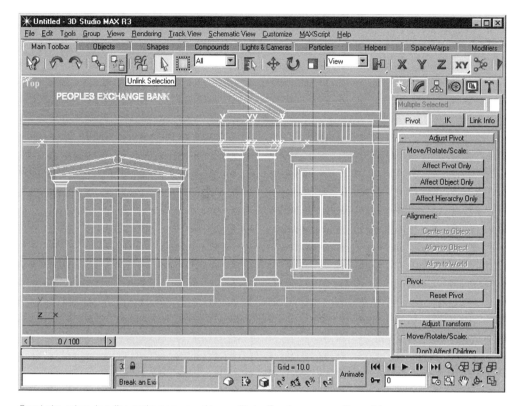

Front view showing the entranceway doors with half columns on either side.

Booleans: to Union or Not to Union

One of two possible schools of thought can be applied here. You can make two cylinders and perform two Booleans and end up with two separate entities (my first choice), or you can select both angled pieces of molding and subtract one cylinder from both, making a single, joined piece.

Since at this point the molding is to be painted one color, it would seem logical to make it as one piece and have fewer pieces that need color applied to them. If, however, the client decides that they want to let the wood grain show (not uncommon on colonial design buildings), then in order to apply a wood map or procedural wood mapping, it will be necessary to break the object into two. This is more work than keeping them separate in the first place.

In AutoCAD, to create a copy of the cylinder on the exact location of the original, choose COPY, pick the first cylinder, pick a random point on the screen, and when you are asked for a second point of displacement, enter the @ symbol. Your copy will occupy the same space as your original and both sides will match identically.

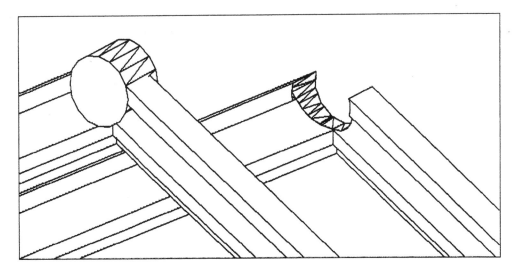

The design cut into the point of the peak above the front door was accomplished by creating the peak as shown earlier for the end view and then subtracting a cylinder from the results of that process.

BEVELED BLOCKS

These tall, thin decorative corner blocks, used on the four corners of the tower (added later by the client), began life as a simple L-shaped outline. They were then extruded 4'. The corners were knocked off with the chamfer command. The same technique is used for the blocks on the corners of the main building but their shapes are a little more complex, as they are in mirror-imaged pairs.

Always draw one of an object and copy it into place. Lock in the axis before you begin to copy the blocks vertically to complete the edge of the tower. This stack can then be copied to the other corners and rotated in 90-degree increments into the final position.

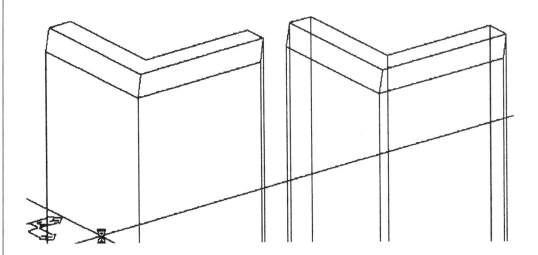

Sometimes a lot of detailed geometry can be had for very little work.

WINDOW CASINGS

The basic shape was found on a millwork sheet in the packet provided by the client. Tracing the outline took a few minutes. (Using the AutoCAD pedit command option, join, it is possible to combine the loose lines and circle segments into a single closed pline entity, necessary for extruding.) The shape is then extruded.

The cross section is common to both the front and side windows in this project. You can either copy the profile before extruding it or you can extrude it to the longest (tallest) casing required and cut the excess off later for the shorter window casings.

Using AutoCAD, there are three methods for trimming the excess length from a solid (stretch doesn't work with solids in AutoCAD). One method is to copy the piece on top of itself, move the copy into the appropriate position and use the subtract command using the copy as a tool to remove the excess. Sometimes, because of scale, this isn't the best option. You can also create a box (as in the peak exercise) and use it to subtract the excess. A third alternative is to make the extrusion using the shortest segment needed, copy it onto itself, move the copy upward until the desired height is achieved and then (in most cases) union the segments together into a new whole.

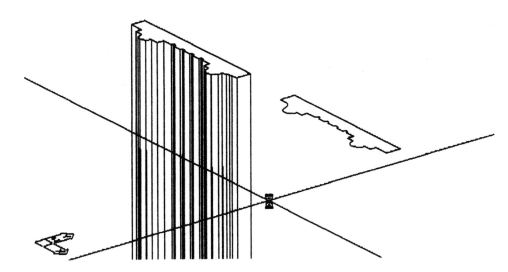

The complexity of the geometry is determined by how close the camera will come to that that detail. The farther away the camera, the lower the level of detail. This piece of window casing will be one of the closest pieces of geometry to the camera and therefore is drafted and extruded in the greatest possible detail. If at a later date this were to be mapped with a wood grain or procedural wood material, it would be visually complex and interesting.

Using MAX, the profile is traced and extruded. Changing height is easier in MAX, as you simply move the location of the end vertices (modify/suboject/vertex/select-move). Window and door headers, decorative moldings, window and door sills are all made using this method.

THE POLYGONAL FACE

All surfaces in AutoCAD and 3D Studio MAX (and most other 3D generating packages) are represented by three-sided polygons. These polygons can have visible or invisible edges. In most cases the invisible edges are best left that way. When they come over from AutoCAD and become unintentionally visible, they can add quite a bit of confusion to the screen image. When you want to turn them on (or off if they are visible and you need them hidden), perhaps to determine if a hole in a model is a missing face, use the modify, subobject edge selection, select the entire entity and use autoselect. Depending of the shape of the model, it may be necessary to try various angle settings to make them disappear or become visible at will.

HIDDEN EDGES

When models from AutoCAD are passed to 3D Studio MAX, the edges that were hidden in AutoCAD suddenly become visible. This can be corrected but in most cases the procedure is not worth the time. When these surfaces are rendered, the seams usually disappear except on very large, flat surfaces where they are sometimes incorrectly interpreted and each one is shaded differently.

When flat surfaces are incorrectly interpreted, you will have to hand edit the smoothing groups so that the surfaces are treated as one. This is accomplished by using the modify, edit mesh, subobject

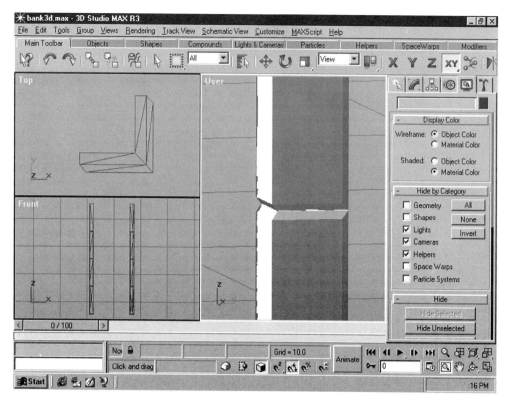

Lines that cut across flat planes sometimes appear on models coming from CAD programs to 3D Studio MAX. In most cases you can ignore them.

face, smoothing groups options, selecting the two offending faces, and giving both faces the same smoothing group value. See the MAX User's Guide for a full explanation.

CHAPTER 12 PEOPLE

PEOPLE IN ARCHITECTURE

Architects and the illustrators who produce their visuals have always included people to give the viewer a sense of scale.

The male and female figures in an illustration can affect the mood and atmosphere of a piece as well as lend a certain ambience or lack of it depending in whether they are walking, sitting, standing casually, talking, or running.

The clothing on a character can set the mood of a place (formal, casual, wealthy, middle-class, working-class, poor) faster than any other single element.

THE MALE FIGURE

I selected characters from the www.3dcafe site and modified them for my purpose. This bank is in a rural part of Kentucky. I felt it inappropriate to have the male in a suit; blue-collar slacks and shirt on the male seemed most appropriate.

I wanted the scene to tell a story. I staged him to look comfortable in the environment and therefore had him walking casually toward the front door. He would arrive first and could get the door for the lady, who would arrive second.

Be sure you always read the copyright notices on the use of another illustrator's models and give credit where it is due.

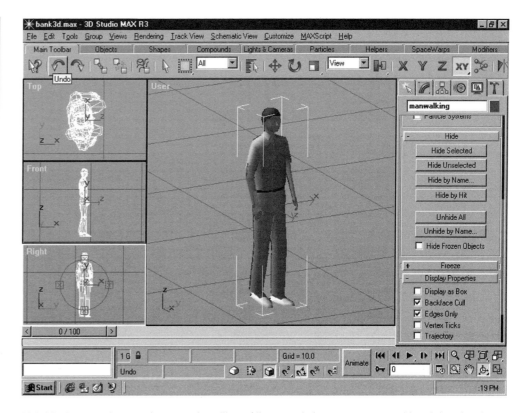

Height, dress, posture, gestures, and position of the people in your scene must be determined on a picture-by-picture basis. The more you can say with these elements, the less you have to talk about your work; your message will convey itself.

THE FEMALE FIGURE

The female figure I downloaded from the www.3dcafe.com site was out of proportion. The head was too small, the legs too long and, as my wife pointed out, the hem of the dress was uneven and too long, and the chest was exaggerated. After resculpting most of the body, she was ready to represent the middle class of this rural Kentucky town.

By placing her in the foreground and in scale as a 5′ 7″ tall woman, the rest of the scale of the bank was established. The color of her dress, hair and shoes were chosen to complement the colors of the bank. Everything in an illustration must be an intentional compositional element, whether color, shape, line, form or shade. This is, after all, art and everything contributes to the final impression.

If you want to do more exotic things with your people I suggest Poser or People for People (for 2D models). These commercial products have withstood the test of time and work well with the associated plug-ins to MAX such as Clothes Reyes and Character Studio.

People have always been an integral part of illustration for architecture. Using them well, rather than just dropping them into a picture, can lend more than scale to your work.

PLANNING AHEAD

Thinking ahead to the desired finished product in your sketches or your mind's eye, visualize cars, trees, grass, cement retainers and curbs, and blacktop or macadam with parking space stripes. We are close to completion of our model.

We need to begin to think out the topography of large areas such as the parking lot. I choose to avoid these areas until late in the modeling process because if they are defined early, they set the extents of the drawing well outside the detailed building area and add an extra zoom in step to each zoom extents.

We must establish how we want to stack things up. The plane on which the model sits will be macadam or blacktop. This way the cement curb will sit on top of that, well manicured grass that is edged precisely will rise above that, and the concrete foundation of the building will bring us to the first course of brick which we have already created.

Once these elements are established, we can determine where to place the feet of our people, the tires of the cars, the bases of the trees, and the mountain in the background.

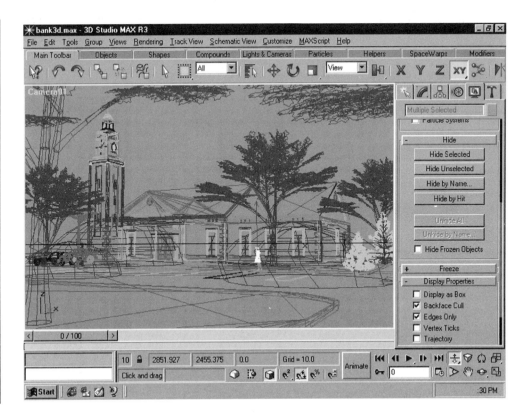

Step back and review where you are going. Review your initial sketches and notes about halfway into a model to help you avoid missing small details considered important by the client. This can also help you keep in mind the appropriate level of detail as you model.

NOTE: This particular community had one small mountain which would be seen behind the bank. It was considered important to use photos of this mountain to establish location, therefore some time was expended matching the look of that specific feature.

CHECKING YOUR VIEWS FREQUENTLY

A quick check on the end view shows that our car tires are sunk 6" into the roadway and that both our people are floating at different heights above the ground. Easily corrected but overlooked simple details, if allowed to go to print at $25 per square foot, can be very expensive.

Note that some of the model seems to have disappeared. Use the hide features to put away geometry that doesn't need to show in order for you to continue your work. You will find this progressively more important as the sizes of your models increase, and the time you spend waiting for your models to redraw increases proportionally with size.

NOTE: The unseen tires have been removed on the far side of the car from the camera to keep down the size of the model.

It is a commonly used trick, in order to ground objects, to sink them slightly (1/2" or so) into the surface they stand on. This will help establish the illusion of the object being on the surface, rather than disconnected from it or floating over it.

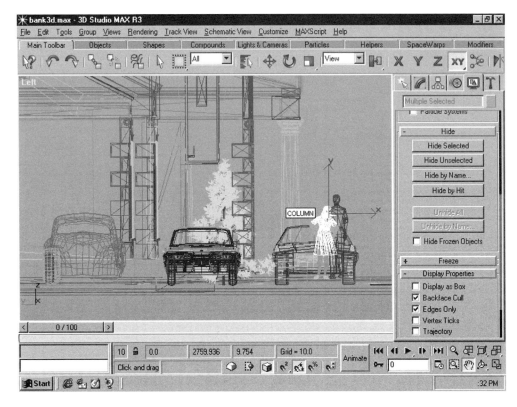

Having things at the proper height above the ground is important. Floating people and cars sunk into the road surface don't help the illusion of realistic rendering.

CHAPTER 13 LETTING THE ARTIST LOOSE

ARTISTIC LICENSE

Sometimes the location of existing trees is given. You may be provided with a landscape plan as well. If this is the case, you lose control over using bushes and trees to hide undesirable elements or frame your picture.

Shadows can become a powerful element in framing the building or the entire illustration. In the case of buildings lacking interesting texture, the light passing through the trees can be usedto create patterns and turn a dull building into an interesting visual and still maintain the extreme accuracy that is desirable in architectural illustration.

The cars shown here were also complements of the contributors to the www.3dcafe.com site. I have Datapoint Labs automobile sets containing much newer cars. However, I was told that this location was not high-income and felt that older cars might lend more of credibility. The car color was chosen to enhance the overall color scheme and composition. Unnecessary elements on the side of the cars facing away from the camera were stripped away but copies of the original, unedited cars were stored in a stock parts library I maintain under the (creatively chosen) subdirectory heading of cars.

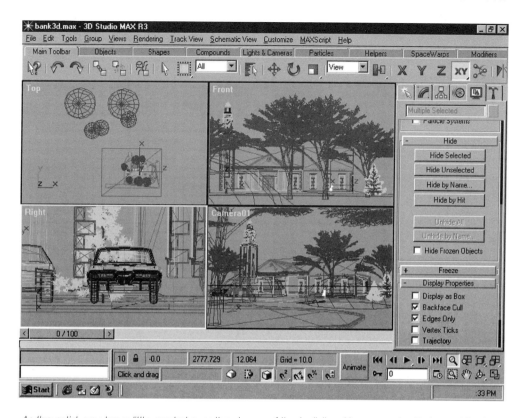

As the artist, you have little control over the shape of the building. Your opportunity to contribute to the mechanical composition of the drawing may be limited to the placement of the light sources to lead the viewer's eye with the shape of the shadows.

ENVIRONMENT

The environment in which the building is placed varies with each illustration. A ground plane can be instantly established using a simple box entity in MAX. The curbs, walkways, and islands that will establish the shape of the parking areas, as well as irregular-shaped grassy areas, are best created using splines and extrusion in AutoCAD or MAX.

This building has handicapped entry in the form of a ramp that parallels the front of the building. (You created this ramp earlier.) If it is necessary to modify the bottom of this ramp, it is easy to grab the vertices on the low end and pull them down to the ground level once it is established. If you had noted this decision in your job notebook, you would have had a reminder to do it at this time.

Parking stripes can be created with simple planes or patches assigned a white or yellow color, depending on local codes. I chose to use a thin box instead. It has been my experience that simple planes tend to get lost in the rendering unless they are raised a slight distance off the macadam; if they are raised too high, they create strange shadow effects. You can use a plane and turn off CAST SHADOWS for these objects to avoid the shadow effect.

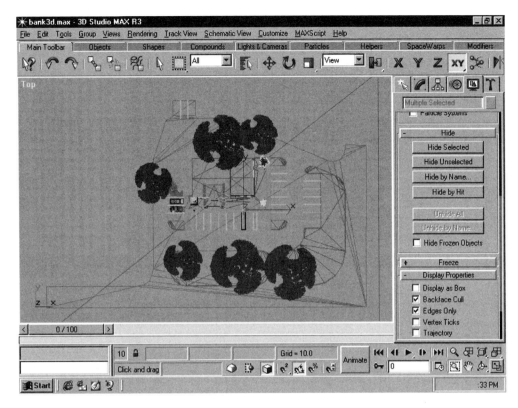

Some special considerations must be given to handicap ramps in the concrete planning and layout of the parking lot striping and symbols; check with the architect to be sure these are correct before proceeding.

Be certain that you establish the space requirements for the handicapped parking spaces and use the standard handicapped parking symbols available on the second disk of your 3d Studio MAX disk set under shapes.

WALKING THE PERIMETER

The concrete slab that forms the base of the building and tower were available on a separate drawing. The elements were not drawn perfectly: There is a slight mismatch between the building base and the concrete shape.

By starting a spline at one corner where they did match and continuing completely around the perimeter of the building, it was easier to create a new, closed spline shape to extrude the concrete base rather than trying to correct the original drawing.

By creating a block to cut out the stairs from the concrete base using a Boolean subtract, the foundation and stairs were created in minutes.

Using the chamfer command (AutoCAD only), and again moving around the perimeter segment by segment, it was easy to knock off the top corners to create a bevel all around the edges and a sharp reveal line that enhanced an otherwise dull chunk of cement.

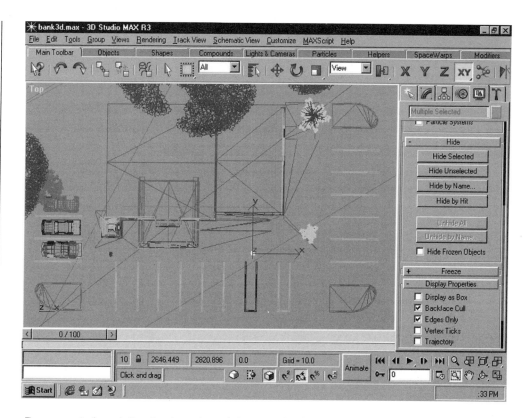

The concrete foundation, front porch and steps are simple elements. Often, chamfering the top edge about one or one and a half inches can lend a nice shadow line or reveal the edge of an otherwise dull chunk of gray material.

I decided to raise the grass 2" above the edge of the curb; at other times, it was desirable to drop the grass below the curb. To create this effect quickly, do the following: After establishing the spline to define the shape of the island, copy and then scale down the copy 4", make a second copy on top of the first, then extrude both the outer and one of the inner plines together about 6". Subract the inner from the outer, extrude the inner spline 4" and assign it a grass.

EDGE HANDLING

AutoCAD and MAX handle intersecting planes from different objects differently. If one object is sunk into another, there's no actual line where the two objects intersect that has been calculated within the geometry. AutoCAD sometimes has a problem representing this situation.

In MAX those intersections are established and rendered perfectly. Here the sections were drawn to be much thicker than necessary; at assembly, they were too thick. Sinking them into the face of the brick sections to the proper depth created clean edges.

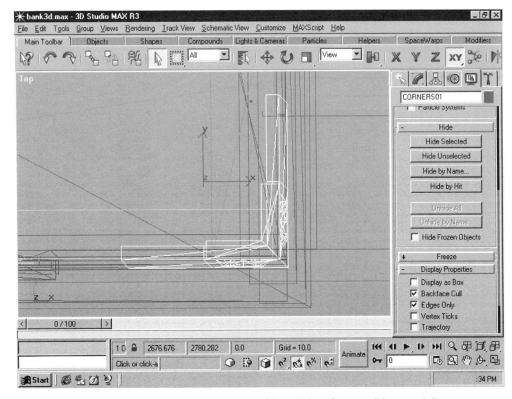

These decorative pieces were built to set on top of the brick surface; as it turns out, they were much too thick. Simply sinking them into the surface of the brick wall would have caused unpredictable results in AutoCAD, but renders flawlessly in MAX.

Since the sections do not intrude into the interior, if a walkaround of the interior takes place later, they will not show. This is a visually confusing situation. Turning off the hidden faces, or having each of the elements show in a different color, will make handling the parts and differentiating the elements easier.

ALIGNMENT

At this point in the model, it is probably best to make the concrete match the building. Check to be sure that your concrete base and building footprint align properly front, back, and both sides. When the CAD drawings are done by different people and at different times there may be discrepancies.

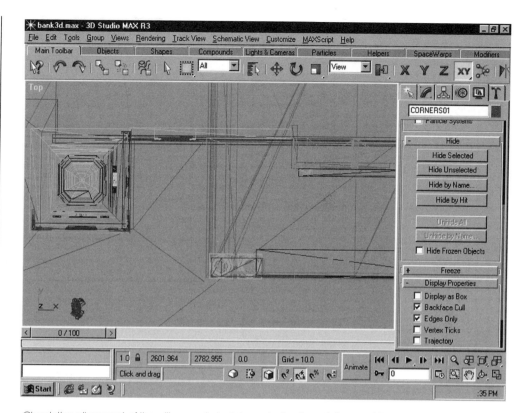

Check the alignment of the pillars and clock tower to the foundation and the alignment of the depth of the window elements to the wall. Glass panels must be in or behind the mullion segments.

CHECK ALIGNMENT

The pillars and clock tower represent elements that must align individually with the foundation corners and edges in order to look correct. Zero in on each of these areas. Depending on their location of the light sources, it can cast strange shadows and make your model look incorrect if the alignment is not exact.

Note the half columns' alignment with the face of the wall where they meet; any apparent small space here will look sloppy.

A simple method you can use to correct these problems is by using the MAX modify subobject, vertex option. Work in the plan view, with the appropriate restraint (x or y in this case) selected; move the incorrect vertices vertically and horizontally as required.

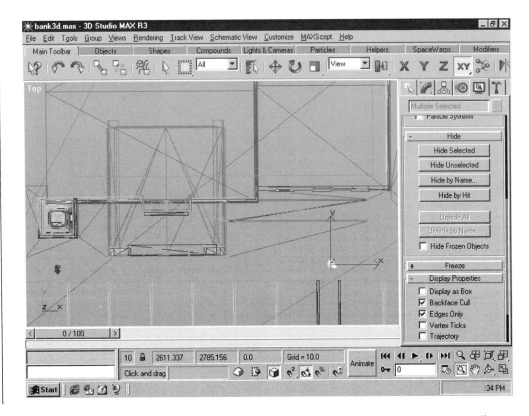

Getting the building and foundation in line with each other may be simple or cost you a half hour. If they are not aligned, they will not render properly and you will not have a professional finished product.

ALIGNMENT OF DIAGONALS

The tower is now made up of many segments. Look in plan view and inspect the various bevelled edges that meet to form this shape. The diagonals must align properly. One method of checking is to create a line, lock the rotation to fixed increments (say 5° (see units)), rotate the line to 45° and move it around as a gauge. You may want to set two: one at 45°, the other at -45° as shown.

Make sure the decorative or logo elements of the bank are sunk into the faces of the tower equally front and side. Improper placement of the clock elements will cast unrealistic shadows later. Be sure their relationship with surrounding surfaces are also correct.

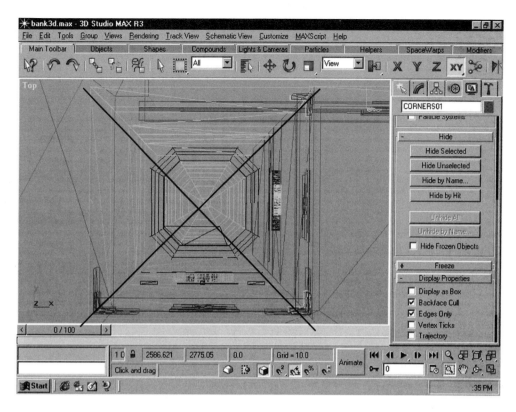

Check the alignment of the diagonals, the seams between the front and right sides of the clock tower and the diagonals of the cupola. Make sure the decorative or logo elements of the bank are sunk into the faces of the tower equally front and side.

FACETED VS. SMOOTH SURFACES

Most standard surfaces (other than nurbs) are built from a series of faces. All these faces are triangular and are usually found in pairs, forming a rectangular face. The number of faces required to create the illusion of a curved surface is directly proportional to the distance away from that surface you are standing (or your virtual camera is placed).

Since the number of surfaces is also directly proportional to the time it takes to render an object, there is a tradeoff between the pursuit of the perfectly smooth surface and the quick rendering model. All programs are designed to give the best approximations according to the programmer's algorithm. That algorithm is not always best for you and your situation.

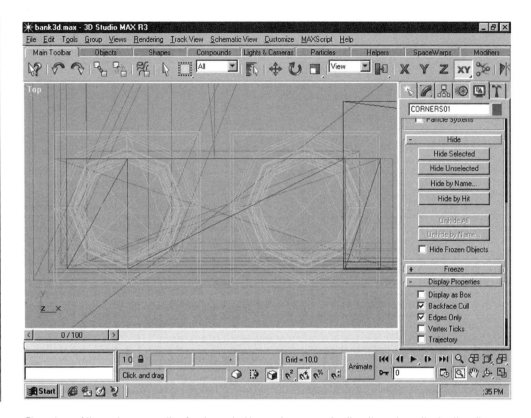

Plan view of the columns on the front porch. Upon close examination they show that rather than being round, they are octagonal. They will render as faceted rather than smooth.

FIXING THE PILLARS

The pillars shown on this page and the next were created in Autocad using the revolve command. When those objects that were solid to that program are exported to MAX through the use of the .DXF export format, some approximation takes place during the translation. If that approximation doesn't give the desired result, you have several choices. One choice is to return to AutoCAD and create a column that has the number of faces you need. In this case the AutoCAD revsurf command can be controlled by setting the surftab1 and surftab2 variables to a value of 20. These settings will give a smooth surface. Or you can redraw the profile using a MAX closed spline and lathe it to form a smooth solid.

The half column against the walls shows the same degree of rough approximation. This would be fine if the model were intended only for animation and the cameras were moving around the model fairly quickly. But in this case, since we're creating a high quality still image, this level of detail is insufficient.

ROUND COLUMNS

Without correction, the column will appear to be an octagon. Its appearance could be greatly improved by selecting the column portions that should look round and assigning all the revolved surfaces the same smoothing group number. In some cases this will be sufficient; try it before rebuilding the object completely.

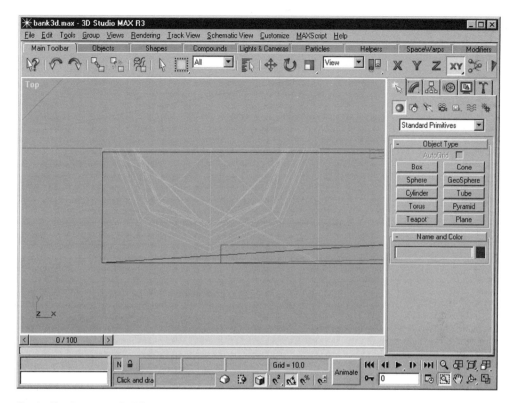

The half column against the wall shows the same degree of rough approximation. This would be fine if the model were intended only for animation and the cameras were moving around the model fairly quickly. But in this case, since we're creating a high quality still image, this level of detail is insufficient.

SMOOTHING GROUPS

The samples on the left show a revolved solid, generated from a pline, with the surftabs set to 6 (the default). By resetting them to 20 the object created using the revsurf command is highly faceted. From a distance this would be acceptable.

By turning on the smoothing feature of the import dialogue box when the object is imported, the image in the upper right, perspective view, appears to be much smoother, almost a continuous surface.

The lower right viewport shows the results of the various treatments of the surfaces.

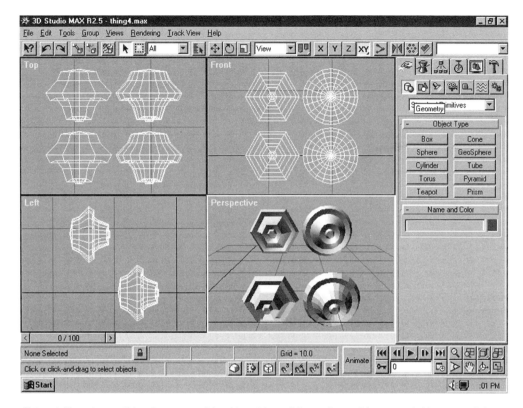

This additional smoothing is accomplished by giving all the adjacent faces matching smoothing numbers. If you haven't read about these in the MAX User's Guide, this would be a good time to learn to use them.

THE CUPOLA

IN MAX

Start with the eight-sided roof shape and work down to the base. By creating an eight-sided gengon (under extended primitives) with 12 segments vertically and then manipulating the faces using an edit mesh, subobject face and selecting every other face vertically, it is possible to use the uniform scale and create the basic object with uneven sides in one simple step as shown.

The remainder of the manipulation required to create the shape is a series of selections made in the front view and scaled uniformly in the plan view until the final shape is achieved.

The window portion is another gengon with eight sides and only one vertical segment. By creating a box and rotating two copies, 120 ° each, and subtracting them from the basic gengon the windows are all cut (remove the remaining faces inside the shape if needed).

The remainder of the construction consists of a pile of box entities, properly scaled and stacked.

NOTE: if you find the Boolean operation causes too much trouble, select an edit mesh operation after each subtraction. This may stabilize the end product.

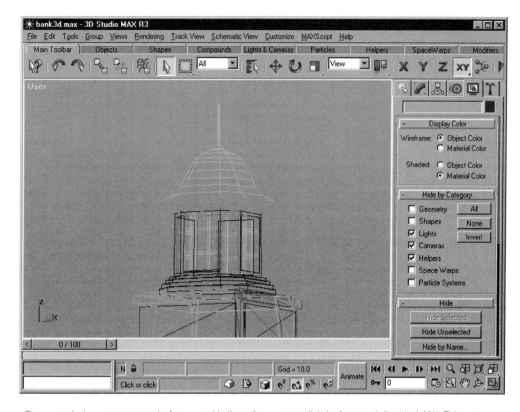

The cupola is a near-organic form and is therefore a candidate for modeling in MAX. This one started life as a gengon with eight sides and twelve segments vertically. The remainder is composed of a Boolean operation performed with blocks on another gendon and a few additional boxes.

VERTEX EDITING

Vertex editing looks difficult to most students. It is in fact the modeling method closest to working in clay that we have in MAX. Moving, scaling and rotating vertices individually, or in carefully selected groups, can form complex shapes very quickly.

The shape that you start with will determine how difficult the end product is to achieve. When you begin using this method, always start with double the number of faces you think you will need; it is easier to reduce them later than to have too few. Adding to the number of faces can be done later by going back to the original object creation level in the stack and increasing the number of faces on any surface. This sometimes yields unexpected results. You can also tessellate by edge or face-center to add more faces to a selected area of your design.

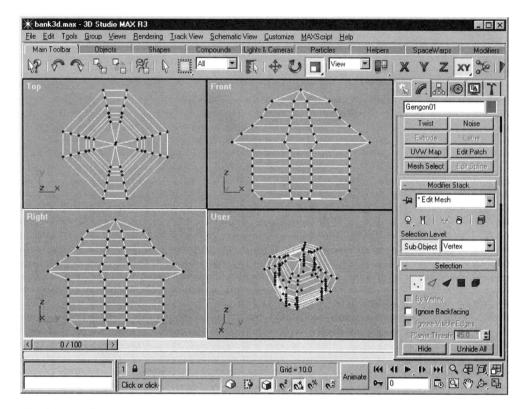

This is the roof of the cupola in process; the groups of vertices are being selected in horizontal rows in the right or front view and being scaled, uniformly, in the top view. Switch views without losing your selection set by right clicking.

LOGO AND CLOCK PARTS

The same approach that was used in Chapter 1 for the company logo text applies to the logo on the face of the clock tower.

The logo was available on the business card of the bank. This was scanned on a flat bed scanner in 16 colors at 600 d.p.i. in the .TIF format. I chose to bring this into Corel Draw and use the auto trace function and export the vector/spline results as a .DXF file. This was brought directly into MAX.

In MAX, extrude each of the outlines and shift each of them to its appropriate level. The first logo is ready to place. Create the other by copying the first and then rotating that copy into place.

The clock consists of a grouping of boxes; the 12, 3, 6, and 9 markers are an array of one simple box object. Try to notice details such as the time of day shown on the clock matching the sun location at that time. 10:30-11:00 would have been a better choice here.

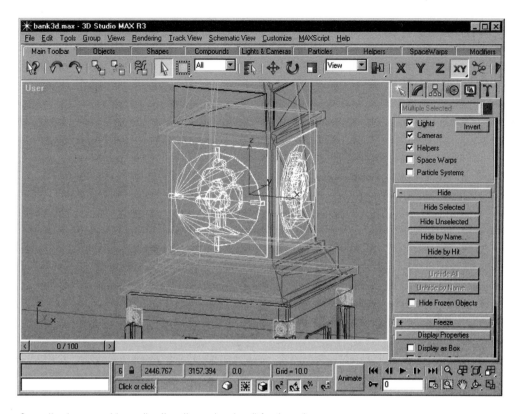

Scan the logo and trace it rather than drawing it freehand.

TOWER DETAILS

The tower has recesses in each face. Each recess has three raised blocks with beveled edges equally spaced up the center. Corner caps with beveled top and bottom edges adorn each vertical corner above the roofline. The first ten feet of the tower has offset L shapes from the ground to the roof height, and each has decorative caps.

These decorative elements are what make this building distinctive. They must be adhered to carefully.

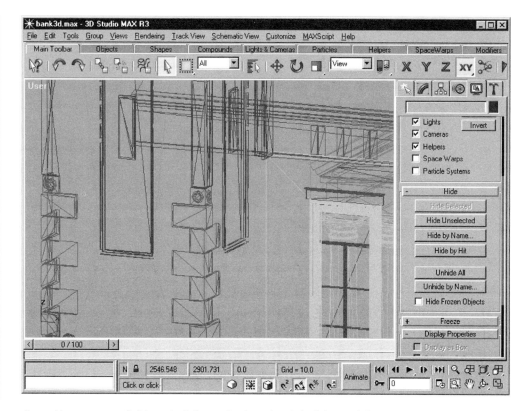

By making one cap (left-handed) then mirroring about (in this case) the vertical axis, you get the reverse part for free (right-hand version).

DECORATIVE CAPS

The decorative caps were created from a BOX entity and a TORUS. The TORUS is sunk halfway into the box. The combination is then copied and rotated 90° and placed so that they form a corner. By selecting the vertices on the top and bottom of the outer edges, it is easy to form the bevel using modify, subobject vertex.

Any amount of practice you can gain with the use of the Shift and Ctrl buttons and an understanding of select by window and select by crossing will make you much more confident modeling by vertex manipulation.

Although the recesses and raised blocks could have been done in a single Boolean operation, it creates a more stable structure to perform several simple operations rather than one complex one. The recess has a moulding along the edges. I chose to create a simple BOX primitive and subtract all the way through. I then built the moulding by extruding a profile along a rectangular path. The back face of the recess is a simple box primitive The raised blocks are box entities with several segments along the edges and by selecting groupings of vertices and scaling them, it is easy to create the illusion of a moulding along the edge.

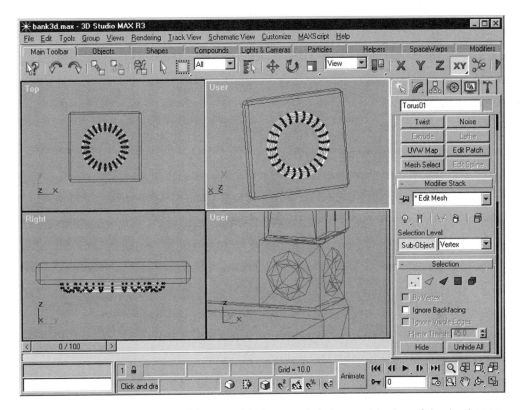

Complex-looking objects such as this corner block are really just a combination of simpler shapes manipulated properly. The half a doughnut is simply a torus primitive sunk into a box.

THE CORNER CAPS

The corner caps were made by extruding a simple single shape. The bevel on top was accomplished by selecting the vertices on the outer edge and using the axis restraints (X,Y or Z), moving them into a new location. The L shaped blocks were made the same way except that after the first one was made it was mirrored, rotated into place and then copied vertically until the correct height was achieved. The original and the copies were grouped. The group was then copied to each corner and rotated accordingly.

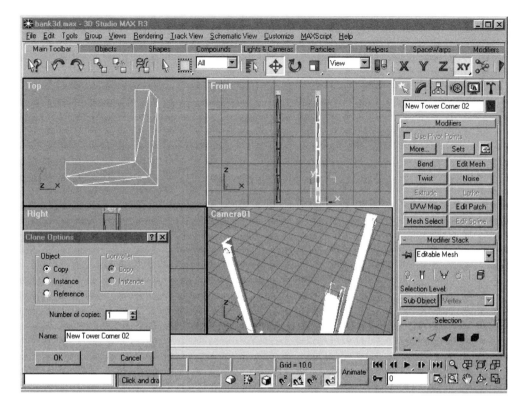

AutoCAD users learned long ago to "Draw it once and copy it forever." Whenever there is an opportunity to create one piece of geometry and reuse it, do so. When you create anything that you can anticipate using again, save a copy into a library.

LOUVER AND FRAME

The louver frame was created as a solid in AutoCAD. When it was translated into MAX it was interpreted by the .DXF translator as an octagonal tube. If the camera were to come close to this object, its crude structure would become evident. In that case it should be replaced with a thin section made from the TUBE primitive in MAX.

The louvers in the frame could consist of a series of horizontal slats about two inches wide and a quarter of an inch thick. There would be about a dozen of them and they would (collectively) represent about 148 additional polygons for each of the four louver frames in the building.

Instead of creating the actual geometry, it is simpler to open a graphic software package and paint a map with the paint color for the building as a background and eleven hori zonal stripes in black representing the shadow edges that the slats would have formed. This can then be mapped to the inner circular area of the lover and creates the illusion of geometry very effectively.

The small, simple map will contribute almost no additional time at rendering.

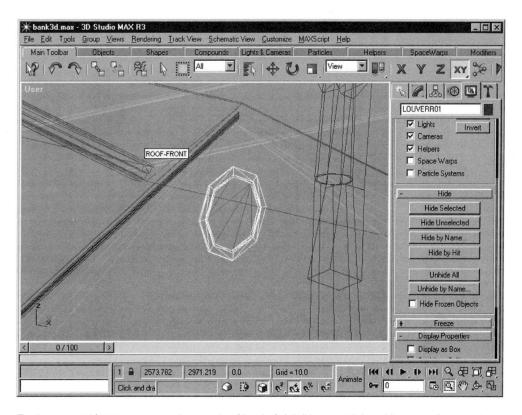

The louver and frame are a good example of level of detail in a model and the use of a map to suggest geometry. The frame is an octagon with a hole in it. The center should have a series of horizontal slats that allow air through for ventilation.

GETTING CLOSE TO THE CAMERA

For those elements that will be close to the camera during rendering or animation, building the full geometry, in detail, is in order.

The corner block L shapes, the decorative cap on top and the details of the window are some of the elements on the model that will be close to the camera.

The pieces of the window were constructed one at a time by extruding the cross section of each piece. The details of the cross sections of this mill-work were provided by the architect.

The header (across the top of the window) is in three separate pieces, the casings (window side pieces), the sill (across the bottom) is in two sections and the mullions (between the panes of glass) are each modeled in full detail.

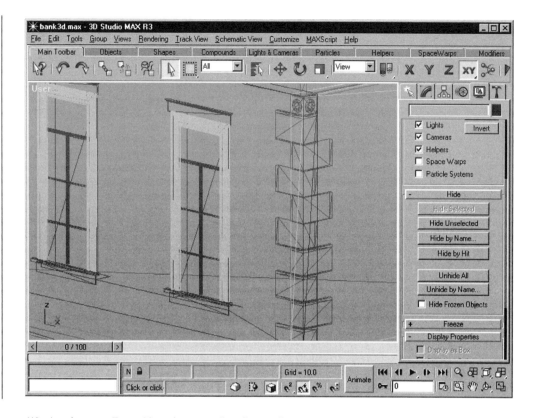

Window frames, sills and headers as well as the mullions are each separate pieces of geometry. Because the camera will pass close to these areas they can not be imitated well with bump maps.

THE GLASS WINDOW MOSAIC

All the panes of glass, collectively, should reflect the scene that they face but not show the (lack of) details inside. When creating the material to be applied to the glass, use panoramic photos of the area to create the illusion of the glass reflecting the actual environment where the building will reside. You may not need transparency at all.

If photos of the area are not available, or the actual area isn't complementary to the building, a map of sky or a stock photograph (available from multiple resources, in digital format) will do.

By making the glass in each window part of a larger piece, the illusion of each pane reflecting part of a greater scene, almost like a mosaic, will enhance the illusion of reality.

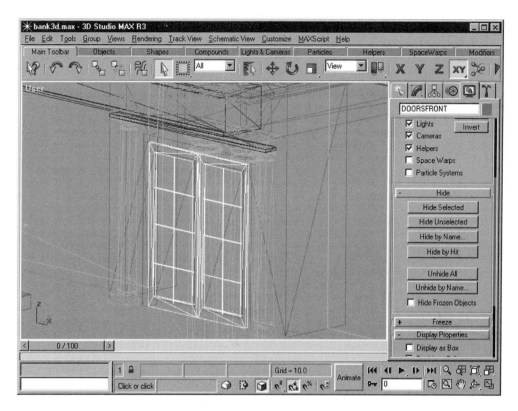

The window glass must hide the internal geometry and interior details and at the same time should reflect the environment, like segments of a mosaic.

BASE PLANES

In the plan view drawings as provided by the architect, there were clear indications of the areas that would be paved with blacktop or macadam. The islands in the parking lot were indicated as well as the grassed-in areas and sidewalks and ramps. The parking lot stripes were also shown clearly and were to be indicated in the final image.

A large box primitive, with the noise material applied (made up of very fine pixels of black and medium grey described earlier) made up the lower-most level of the stack-up.

The outlines of the island areas were converted into lines in AutoCAD but could have been drawn as splines in MAX just as easily and extruded in either program. An offset copy of the line about four inches smaller all around acted as the defining shape for the grass. This shape was extruded about two inches higher than the island borders.

The sidewalk was done in the same outline and extrude manner except that the mapping consisted of noise as a base, and a map was created to add a bump mapped depression every four feet to indicate the expansion joints cut between the segments of sidewalk .

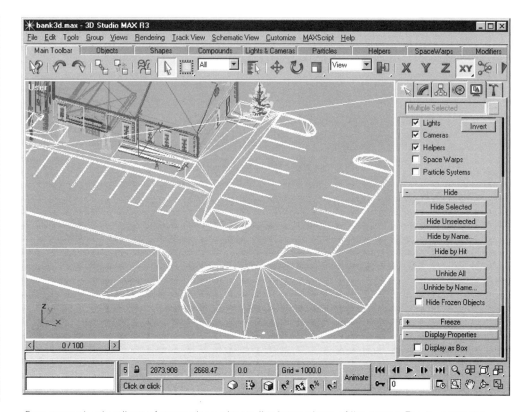

Four separate elevations of geometry make up the base plane of the scene. The lowermost layer is the macadam of the parking lot. The next is the cement that makes up the islands. The third is the grass inside the islands and the fourth is the cement of the sidewalks and the handicap access ramp from the sidewalk to the entranceway slab.

The stripes were originally simple patches. When they rendered, they vanished into the surface they were close to. When they were raised high enough to not get absorbed, they cast a shadow. By right clicking on the patches and shutting off their shadow-casting ability, the problem was solved.

You should be aware of the laws concerning handicapped parking and have the symbols available in a library in 2D, ready to extrude and place on a parking lot striping plan. Fire hydrants and outdoor lights and poles are also useful library items to collect.

TREES AND THEIR SHADOWS

Using the shapes wisely, using trees to cover unwanted elements, indicating the age of the environment with the age of the trees and sculpting the composition by placing trees in front of the light source but off camera are all subtle uses of trees and bushes.

Even when the plan indicates existing or new landscaping, the trees, bushes, and flowers can be elements within your control if you light them and cast shadows with them cleverly.

Trees and their shadows are some of the few compositional elements that illustrators of architectural models have control over.

Have a book on trees at your disposal and collect 3D models of them as often as you come across them.

There is a variety of methods for faking trees. Simple methods include creating a cluster of three intersecting planes and mapping the tree picture and its transparency map on all three planes. If you don't get too close, they can be very effective.

Backgrounds composed of trees can be a simple picture on a patch or multiple layers of pictures on patches. Near-ground or close-up trees need to be 3D models. Many trees are available free off the Web or for a price from Viewpoint DataLabs and similar services.

Always study the architect's photos carefully and/or ask about the trees predominating in the area. You may need maples and a few pines in the North, vice versa in the South.

FINAL COMPOSITION

Nearly finished with all elements in place, trial renderings indicate the pattern on the front lawn is working well visually. It is time to print it and see what it looks like.

I exported a 24" × 18" .TGA format file at 300 dpi and opened it in Corel Photoshop. After scanning the picture carefully with the client, we discovered that there was a problem with the right-side door: One face of the door was a different color than the other. I corrected this problem in both the model and the .TGA file and printed the image as four 8 1/2" × 11" glossy quarters (using the print as tiles feature of the software) and glued them together on a piece of drawing pad cardboard. I used this image as a proof for the client.

The next step was to create a 5,000 × 4,000 × 24 bit image that was used to create a high resolution 5" × 4" color slide. The slide was then used to blow up a photographic image onto glossy photo paper. The framer offered to mount it for a reasonable price.

The image was framed, crated, and shipped. The animation was never created commercially, though I went ahead and rendered the frames and put them on my demo tape for self-promotion.

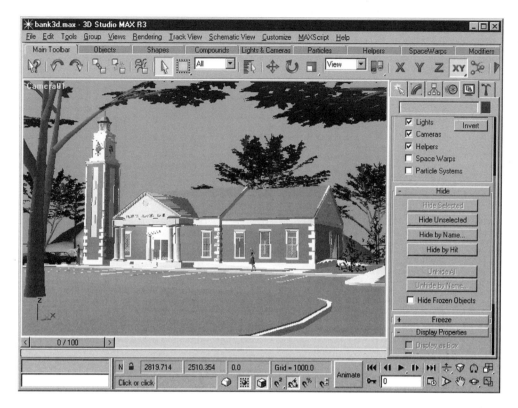

This is the final composition. Cars were added in the background to enhance the sense of scale. The movement around the picture is good except for the foreground, which is too stark. Placing shrubs in the foreground would have obscured the view. Render the final image to see the effect of actual shadows combined with projector light shadows to form a visually interesting matrix on the foreground grass, Note: See the final color illustration in the center of the book.

THE MATERIALS

Architects and interior designers will almost always provide you with more than enough samples of the materials they want used on their models. Simple scanning or procedural materials will provide the full range of surface effects and textures needed for most architectural projects. Alternative resources are magazine pages (be careful of copyright laws), materials on disk that come with products like Corel Draw, PhotoPaint, Adobe Illustrator, and PhotoShop. Collect disks of materials created and sold for demo purposes, old copies of MAX (be careful here—you don't want to have your client spot an overused sky or material map). Additional simple sources are your still camera and your camcorder. Camcorder images can be captured and digitized easily.

CHAPTER 14 CREATING THE ANIMATION FOR THE ACHITECTURAL FLY-AROUND

CAMERA PLACEMENT

The camera placement in this scene was specifically dictated by the client. Architects are very aware of camera angle and eye level location. Average eye level varies with gender and ethnic group. The camera location in this shot is slightly above the eye level of the scaled people in the scene, and angled slightly upward to make the building look bigger than life.

The cone of the camera can be very useful in determining the location of objects, such as trees that might be out of camera view and therefore not necessary except as a source of shadows on on the lawn. Choose a real camera lens size, such as a 35mm, whenever possible to avoid distortion.

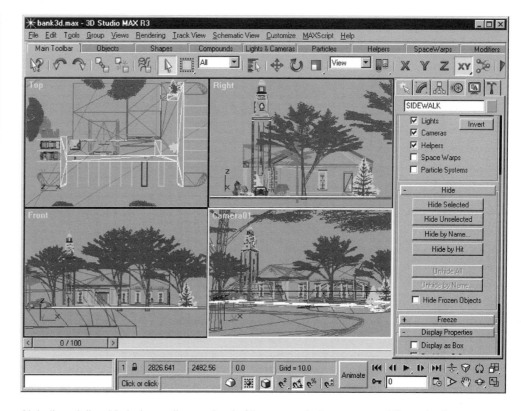

Note the relationship between the eye level of the person in the scene and the actual camera location.

OUTDOOR LIGHTING
CONSIDERATIONS

Outdoor lighting and indoor lighting, day lighting and night lighting, and special effects such as
neon and fluorescent lighting all deserve careful
study. Daylight can usually be recreated with as few
as two lights, one high, warm, bright, shadow
casting target spot and one low, cool, dim, and
non- shadow-casting omni. Nighttime scenes do
best with a little fog in the distance. Set the ambient
lighting to black. Use spots with specific sources (in
other words, a canister on the ground or an in-wall
light to show the source of the light on walls and
walkways).

Indoor lighting, as a general rule, takes many
more light sources to light the scene. Be careful with
omni lights. Always turn on shadow casting or you
will discover a light source burning out your scene
and spend endless hours trying to chase down its
source. Never copy a light in an indoor scene,
always instance it; that way, when you want to
change something about the lighting, intensity,
color, etc., all of the instances change together.

Those lights that light the shadows should
always be cool; those that light the background
should be slightly violet; sunlight and incandescent
lights should be warm; and fluorescent is usually
cool or neutral.

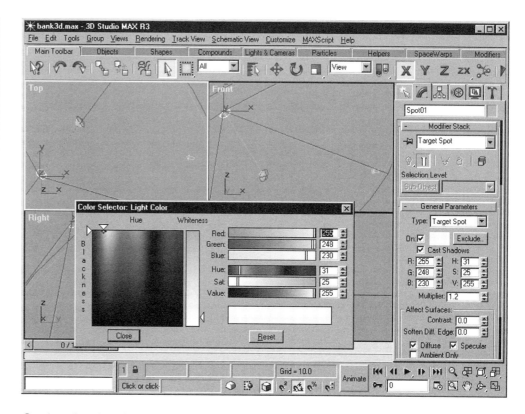

One target spot provides the sunlight; one directional light, cool in color, lights the shadows. There
is one very faint target spot under the entranceway overhang; this light accounts for light that
would be bounced off the entranceway ceiling if Max version 2.5 had a radiosity calculating
feature (which it doesn't).

Time of day, season, weather conditions, latitude, and eclipse
activity all lend a color effect tothe predominating light. Summer
sunsets are the most colorful because of the effects of rising heat and
dust in the air.

Hardware Resources

In the case of this still image, the rendering should be output on your PC. The resulting .TGA file will be about eighty megabytes. This will not fit on a floppy. Actually, it would fit on about 65 floppies if compressed. ZIP cartridges are inexpensive and come in 100 meg capacities. JAZ cartridges hold one or two gig but cost about $75-$150 each. A ZIP cartridge is your best choice here. If you don't own or can't afford a ZIP drive, some service bureaus will lend you a portable external drive. You can send them the file across the Net, but you will need a T1 line and a fast modem for this large size a file.

Post Processing

Camera flares and other special effects can be added by hand or through the use of plug-ins. These are meant as enhancements. Some people are trying to use them as an art medium. Use them with caution and very conservatively. As an example, flares can be added in the Video Post Processor of MAX or they can be added by hand in programs like PhotoShop or Photo Paint using a mask.

Output Devices

There are many options when it comes time to create an approval proof of your work. HP Inkjet technologies have made printers a very inexpensive way to output your final product. Inkjets are wonderful for creating a single 8 1/2″ x 11″ picture as a proof, or you can output the picture in four parts, glue the quarters together to form an 17″ x 22″, and glue it on cardboard for presentation to larger groups at a very low cost and with no travel time.

File Formats for Output

Many formats can be used to output your file. The need for any additional hand touch-up will dictate the use of a raster format such as .TGA, .TIF, or .JPG. When that work is completed, it may be necessary to add text. Text can be added in many raster-based paint programs, but it is better to work with text in a vector-based program because it can be edited later without having to paint out portions of the artwork and/or the artwork can be reinserted if minor changes are made and the text does not have to be recreated. A vector-format file that comes from Corel Draw will have an extension of .CDR A vector-format file from Adobe Illustrator will have a file extension of .AI.

When it comes time to actually bring the file to a printer (for large format output such as 11″ x 17″ or larger), it is best to check with the service bureau that will be processing the file. Some will want it in raster format such as .TGA, and they will manipulate it; this is the case with Fiery and similar processes where the image will be further interpreted by a computer. Some places have their equipment set up to accept files directly from Adobe products in .EPS format.

Time and the Service Bureau

Be aware that service bureaus have a very stringent policy designed to have you get work to them on time. If a job is $100 with seven days' notice, it is $200 with four, and $500 if you want it tomorrow. Planning ahead for printed work can save you the profit on a job. Always begin a job with a phone call to your service bureau and ask three questions: How much will the job cost? Is their equipment in working order? and Will it be available on the date you expect to drop off the job? It is always a good idea to have a back-up location to produce the work if your primary source has a breakdown. The day the job is due is not the time to begin researching an alterative service bureau.

Chapter 15 Delivery and Follow-Up

Late Revisions

Clients, particularly architectural designers, have a habit of showing up at the last minute with "critical" changes that "have" to be incorporated in the animation or still. Don't scrap the whole thing. Often, with a little creativity, the change can be shot separately and post-processed into place. The clone features of PhotoShop and Photo Paint will allow changes to be incorporated into an existing piece. In the case of an animation, changes that are not too major can be faked just by rerunning the frames where the change is in closeup and cutting/editing this back into the remaining animation without correcting the whole piece.

Backing Up Your Projects

You can never make enough copies of your work. Considering that failure to complete a single job can cost you your reputation, it is always a good idea to assume the worst about your storage medium. At the least, you should have a subdirectory on your hard drive where the primary copy of your work is always stored. It is a minimum requirement to have a floppy or ZIP cartridge dedicated to the job at hand. I also maintain a third source on JAZ, just in case the worst happens. Hard drives die at the most inopportune times. If they become corrupted and the corruption transfers to your floppy, having a third copy will no longer look foolish. Most models are under 1.44 meg (the capacity of a floppy); the custom maps can be saved on a second or third floppy.

Save your primary resource material as well. The drawings that you received from the client can often find secondary usage. If you teach, you will find that "real" drawings make the best model material for students. I have never had a client refuse to allow their plans to be used as school resource material. Most take it as a compliment that you want to use their designs.

Back-Up Media

My experience has been good with cartridge-type devices, 3 1/2" floppies ZIP, and JAZ. I have had consistently bad experiences with tape backup devices.

CONCLUSION

In this book, there is enough information about logo creation, mechanical engineering projects and architectural illustration and animation (supported by the documentation that is shipped with MAX, AutoCAD, Adobe PhotoShop or Corel Photo Paint and Adobe Illustrator or Corel Draw) for you to go into the industrial animation world as a contractor.

AutoCAD is a very formal (left-brained) software package in its approach to building models. Precision is called for in mechanical engineering, and AutoCAD provides that precision. Architectural folks will provide drawings in 2D in the AutoCAD format. Working with those drawings and manipulating the data contained in them will yield the most satisfactory results in a model in the shortest period of time.

PhotoShop and Photo Paint are top of the line packages for painting your own backgrounds, material maps and tile. Understanding the manipulation of these programs is essential. You will use them to touch up the finished file before printing as well.

MAX is the center of the suite of tools that you will need to learn to use. Operating MAX is more art than science. Many objects are created by eye rather than formula and the more experienced you are with sketching and drawing freehand, the more success you will have with MAX. There is a hard way and an easy way to do anything in each of these packages, and it is best to familiarize yourself with them to find the shortcuts.

Finally, Corel Draw and Illustrator will become valuable tools to you when it comes to handing text and printable pages. Illustrations in manuals are always accompanied by text, titles and body copy. Your ability to format pages and lay out entire manuals will pay off with larger clients.

It is always best not to get overly technical when discussing software. The client could care less what software, platform, or hardware you use to create their product. Talk shop at user's group meetings with fellow animators, at SIGGRAPH NAB, Autodesk University, E3, Comdex/Windows World, and IEEE, but not with clients. With clients, talk benefits. Illustrations clarify for your clients the form, fit, and function of the design. Animation can provide a feeling of confidence on the part of entrepreneurs about the reality of a design that they can not visualize from blueprints and get closure on shaky deals because nonartistic people can "see" the product.

Illustration and animation are powerful closing tools. With them, you can create powerful presentation material not available through any other resource. You literally create reality in the minds of prospects of all kinds; that is your primary contribution to the marketplace and the perception of the need for your work. Accurate, colorful, well composed and properly executed work will provide you with word-of-mouth advertising, which is the best kind you can get.

To quote Raymond of the www.3dcafe.com website, "Render on."

Appendix A: Vector vs. Raster Graphics

Both vector and raster graphics have a place in the creation of illustrations and animation using computers. Each format has advantages and disadvantages; understanding each is essential to your success.

A *raster* or *pixel format file* contains a list of dots, their color and location. Each dot is located relative to the upper left-hand corner of the picture. The color of each dot is described in terms of its RGB color and, in some formats, its alpha channel or relative transparency is also documented. Because it is a dot-by-dot description of the file, it is said to be of fixed resolution. Reading the file in a word processor will give no indication of what is in the picture. You can get no information until a paint program interprets it and paints it on a monitor or printed page. Common sources of raster files are Adobe PhotoShop and Corel Photo Paint. Common extensions of raster files are .GIF, .TIF, .TGA, and .BMP.

Vector files contain a description of the geometry of an image. Each piece of geometry that makes up an image is described as a shape on the picture plane. Each piece of geometry is assigned an area of the file and contains a list with the name of the geometric shape described using vectors and scalars (such as a circle is described by its centerpoint location and a radius value). The file records its color, linetype (if the shape has an outline, transparent if it doesn't show) and, depending on its source, other information such as edge feathering and transparency. If these files are opened in a word processor, many of them can be read in English; words such as *circle, line, arc*, etc. make up a large part of the file. Because these files are a description of shapes, they can be scaled to any size without loss of detail; they are said to be resolutionless. Common sources of vector files are Adobe Illustrator, AutoCAD, ProEngineer, and Corel Draw. File formats which are vector based are .DWG, .AI, .DXF, and .EPS.

Most vector-based packages can also hold raster-based information. Raster-based information is not improved by being embedded into a vector file; it is simply transported. Corel Zara is a software package designed to handle both vector and raster graphics on the same page.

When it becomes necessary to print an image in raster format, at a higher resolution than the resolution at which it was scanned or painted, the quality of the output is degraded. Several solutions or algorithms have been created that attempt, with more or less success, to resolve this problem. Resizing will apply a simple math formula to increase the size of the image. To increase the file size by a factor of two, it will simply double the existing pixels side by side and top to bottom. The image is doubled in size and usually halved in quality. Resampling programs came later; their sampling algorithms are more complex, slower to operate, create much larger files, and give a noticeably better image but still not a great product. Raster Image Processing software (RIP software) will increase the size of a file through complex calculations, often appearing to add detail where none existed. The output from a RIPing operation is noticeably better than the other options and is correspondingly more expensive. RIP software and hardware (often dedicated Silicon Graphics Indigo machines) can run $10,000 to $100,000. No matter what the process, three to four times scaling up of any file is usually enough to turn it into unacceptable mush.

Where large-format final images are required, another option is film. It is possible to create continuous tone slides or color transparencies or color positives directly from the raster file. Using this process, the file is processed on a high-resolution screen and shot with a camera onto a 35mm slide or larger (5" × 4") color positive. The slide is then blown up using photographic methods and the result is superior to all other methods of increasing the size of an image. The slide may have a $50 to $150 fee associated with its creation. The first print may run $30 per square foot. These images are usually laminated on a backer board because some of the surfaces are water soluble or subject to finger-print damage. A single 2-foot × 3-foot image can cost you $800 and take several days.

HP600 series or Cannon B.C. series printers are workable for proof-ing your work. For commercial customers they can be used for the finished image on typewriter size paper A (8 1/2″ × 11″). Larger images such as B (17″ × 11″), C (22″ × 17″), and D (34″ × 22″) size sheets can be printed, at a reasonable quality, on a wide body printer such as an HP 6400 series. The service bureau will bill you for the printing service at a rate of $10 - $25 per square foot. Prints are subject to fingerprints both before and after they are processed and must be handled with white, lint-free gloves. Mounting and laminat-ing are recommended if they are going to be passed around a boardroom table and/or handled by people not accustomed to respecting printed surfaces. One of these prints left in direct sunlight, in the back seat hot car, can loose 20 percent or more of its color intensity in a single day.

APPENDIX B: THE PANTONE COLOR SET

If I pull out my oil paints and paint a wide stroke using Cadmium Red Light on a piece of clay surface white paper and then shine a bright incandescent light on it, I will see red. If I take a standard red gel and place it in front of a stage light and shine it on a standard projector screen, I will have red also. If I were to compare these reds to the brightest red on a TV screen or the brightest reds on a computer monitor I would find each of them was a different red. The processing of scanning images, manipulating them on the computer monitor, printing them on our inexpensive CMYK printers and having the finished product printed on a commercial press has made us all very color conscious. Seldom will you find a match between these color sources. Complex calibration systems have been created to coordinate these diverse sources of color. You must make yourself aware of them and use them.

One of the most commonly used systems created to assure consistency between printed media is the Pantone Color Matching System. This system is based on the CMYK (Cyan, Magenta, Yellow, and Black) printing ink standard. The color standard used on TV (NTSC or National Television Standards Committee) or the colors seen on your computer monitor are based on the RGB (Red, Green, Blue) standard. Translating between color systems is easy. Whether you are working with a company's logo or wall paint you will find this system useful.

The translation can be done by hand as follows: Look up the PMS color in PhotoShop; select that color; write down the RGB equivalent value; open MAX; open the material editor; plug the RGB numbers into the color selector window, and apply.

Appendix C: Basic AutoCAD Commands

The following commands are essential to using AutoCAD effectively as a modeling tool. The complete package is useful to learn; it can take many years. Use this as a beginner's guide to kick-start your use of this powerful tool.

2D COMMANDS

LINE to draw simple lines that may be combined later into more complex objects

CIRCLE to draw basic circles and to be used later to create radii and fillets

TRIM to remove a piece of a line or circle segment where it intersects another entity

EXTEND to lengthen a line until it contacts another entity

OFFSET to make a copy at a fixed distance from the original

COPY to make an exact duplicate of an existing object

MOVE to move an object

PLINE to draw a line that can be connected to other lines; a shape must be a polyline to extrude into a 3D object

PEDIT to modify a polyline or to join loose segments into a closed polyline before extrusion

3D ARRAY to make copies in a radial or matrix like pattern

ERASE to delete an object or objects from the drawing

3D COMMANDS

BOX forms a regular six-sided object in 3D space

CYLINDER forms a round solid tube with flat ends

SPHERE forms a sphere

ROTATE3D more versatile than its 2D partner

UCS user coordinate system; defines the current working surface

VPOINT lets you see things in a point of view other than plan or straight on; a useful or starting view point is (1.-.75,.5)

VPORTS allows more than one view of an object on the screen at one time; four is practical

BOOLEAN OPERATIONS

SUBTRACT removes part of one object by using a second as a tool

UNION joins two or more objects into a single entity

INTERSECTION finds and keeps the part(s) of two or more objects where they share or overlap in space

APPENDIX D: EXPORT AutoCAD TO MAX

Although MAX 2.5 and up can read AutoCAD .DWG files directly, there is a loss of control in this procedure. The following description of how to prepare files for .DXF-type translation also applies to preparing the AutoCAD file to be saved in AutoCAD and then opened in MAX directly.

Getting the .DXF (Drawing Exchange Format) file out of AutoCAD so the AutoCAD information can be used in other programs is a simple process. By typing the command dxfout at the command prompt, the program begins to prompt you for a name of the file and (the program will add the .DXF extension) the number of decimal places of accuracy required (the default is six and I don't suggest changing it). A dialog box then opens asking you how you want to output the file. This is the critical step for a file: It can be output using several different criteria to determine the grouping of items as they are saved.

MAX 3.0 has no layering system. Therefore layers, which are so important to the creation of items in AutoCAD, must be converted to something else. The options in the dialog box offer color, layer, and by object.

If each item in the AutoCAD drawing has been assigned a different color, regardless of layer, it will import into 3D Studio MAX as one object per color, i.e., six colors on six items will yield six independent items in MAX. It also means that if you have 150 pieces of plumbing pipe all over a building, all on the same layer, and all the same color, when they import into MAX they will be one object. This one object concept is very useful if you will not be moving any one object and

you want to have them all white PVC plastic. If you want to open doors as you pass through them with a camera during a later animation and you import them all as one object, you will spend a great deal of time detaching each door you wish to open later. This method is usually chosen when a model has been created all on the same (usually the "0") layer and the whole assembly has few pieces, usually a dozen or so. This method has a limit of 256 colors (the AutoCAD color limitation). Each item will import with a number rather than a useful name.

If the by-layer option is chosen, the same type of rule applies. if you place every item that must act independently on its own layer, each item will come into MAX as a separate item. These objects also assume an object name that corresponds to the layer they were on at the time of export. There is no limit to the number of layers you can create and if you choose your names carefully, you will make selection of components in MAX much easier later.

Export by object is a last resort. Use it either for very small files (that have only a few objects) or very large files (where the file will be broken up to be worked on by several people). This method ignores colors and layers and creates a new entity in MAX for each 3D object in the AutoCAD scene. The objects assume an alphanumeric name which tells you nothing about the object. Each object must be selected and assigned a color individually and mapped separately. Release 2.0 and 3.0 of MAX has a feature, for the first time in the history of the 3D Studio programs, to directly import a .DWG (AutoCAD native file) into MAX. The filter is very effective and produces a very stable, useable file. It has several advantages over the .DXF format and may eventually replace it, but the older format will persist for a long time.

Glossary

.3DS The extension of files from the older versions of 3D Studio.

.AI The file extension of a vector, Adobe Illustrator file.

.AVI The extension of a raster video file.

.BMP The extension of a windows raster graphic file.

.DWG The extension of a vector file of a drawing from AutoCAD.

.DXF The extension of a drawing exchange format file; many possible sources, but probably AutoCAD.

.EPS The extension of an encapsulated Post Script file, usually from Adobe Illustrator; it can contain both vector and raster information.

.JPG The extension of a JPEG, raster file. This is the most frequently encountered extension on the World Wide Web. It is a lossy compressed format.

.MAX The extension of a file from MAX by Discreet.

.PRN The extension of a vector-based printer file, often HPGL (Hewlet Packard Graphic Language).

.TGA The extension of a Targa file; format is raster and proprietary to True Color Corporation.

.TIF The extension of a tagged image format, raster file. This is probably the most common file format in use. It is the format used by fax machines to communicate.

.WAV The extension of the most common audio file; this format is recognized by the Personal Video Recorder System.

24-bit color Refers to the number of colors that were saved with the file, 16.7 milion in the case of 24-bit (a chart of the standards will be included in a later book in this series).

35-mm lens The most common camera lens. The human eye at rest looking at a distant object uses approximately a 43.456mm lens curvature, the default of the MAX cameras.

A

Algorithm A mathematical equation used to interpret data.

Amortize To spread the cost of something over a period of time, such as buying a computer you expect to last two years and calculating your cost of doing business per year, using half the total cost each year.

Animatic A rough preview of a movie or animation used to check timing, camera angle, and other elements of the finished product.

Annotation Notes added to a file or document intended to give information about the file but without being a part of the file content. May include date, job name, or other information about the job or artist.

Archival document A copy of a working document kept for purposes of securing the copy against loss. The copy may be stored in a fire-proof box or at another physical site.

Array Copies of an object created at fixed distances or number of degrees apart; may be rectangular, radial, 2D or 3D.

Art director The individual in any graphics business who has the overview of all subprojects that lead to the final project.

As-built Refers to a procedure, usually enacted after the completion of a project (particularly architectural). An individual or group of individuals will confirm that the project was built to the blueprints or they will create dimensioned drawings of a structure where none exists.

Assembly procedure Written or drawn documents, usually created by a project designer in conjunction with representatives from manufacturing that define, in great detail, the assembly of a project.

Assembly tool Any document or physical tool created to aid a specific assembly in a manufacturing environment.

AutoCAD A vector-based Computer Aided Design software package used heavily by engineers, architects, and other professionals that contract illustration and animation.

Autotrace A function of some vector-based programs that will seek the boundary of value areas in a raster image and define them as closed spline shapes. Useful in tracing the shape of a logo or icon and then refining the trace for extrusion into a 3D shape.

Axis   A central line about which a shape is revolved or rotated.

B

Back light   A light used to create a contrast to the direct light in a scene. This is often a cool color, in contrast to a warm direct light, and usually not as bright.

Balloons   Circles used in cartoons to hold text and assign it to a particular character.

BETA-SP   Highest quality BETA tape.

Bid   Follows a proposal in the chain of events leading to a contract, P.O., or letter of intent. It often contains a simplified description of the job, the price, and terms.

Bill of materials   Essentially a list of the parts that make up an assembly. The list often refers to other parts by name and/or part number and is used to assemble all the documents that make up the complete manufacturing package. An understanding of this document chain is essential to dealing with engineering assemblies and animation.

Blend   A third curve, often in three-dimensional space, used to join two other curves in a machined or plastic part where a sharp edge is undesirable.

Blueprint (or blackprint)   Documents created from a translucent mylar or vellum by a simplified photographic process. The basic document by which engineers and architects transmit information.

Boolean   Any one of three results that can occur from the interaction of two or more 2D areas or 3D objects consisting of either subtract, union, or intersect.

Boolean2   A new and improved MAX function (*see* Boolean).

Business forms   Any printed, standardized document blank that you use for your business. The most important of these forms are the letterhead, envelope, business card, fax header, contract, or letter of intent (which may also contain a bid and proposal option).

C

Cabinetmakers   Someone who does precise work with wood, laminates, and related materials. They are highly precise and specialized artisans.

CAD   Computer Aided Design, sometimes generalized to include Computer Aided Design and Drafting.

Camera flare   An undesirable glare effect caused by the infinitely fine grind scratches in a camera lens and the lens coating. Rendering packages can reproduce camera effects without these star-shaped white spots so of course someone wrote an add-on to put them back into computer-generated images to make them look more real.

Camera path   A straight line, circle, arc, or spline curve that a camera is attached to and follows from start to finish as the scene is played out in the computer.

Camera view   What the camera will show at rendering is represented in this selectable view in the rendering or CAD package. It is the view that would be seen through a lens as opposed to a perspective or isometric view.

Capsule   An extended primitive shape that eliminates a lot of work when used to create shapes that are basically cylindrical but need rounded instead of square ends.

Casing   Vertical trim on a door or window.

Cast shadows   Sharp edged shadows caused by one object blocking the light from reaching the surface of another object.

CD   Compact disk.

Chamfer   A clipped edge, as opposed to a fillet or rounded edge.

Chamfer box   A box object created with all edges chamfered.

Cherry-picker   A piece of equipment consisting of a retractable arm with a bucket on the end of it, big enough to hold and lift a person and camera into the air above a scene for aerial or high-angle shots.

Chuck   The gripping portion of the business end of a drill. Holds the drill bit, usually tightened with a chuck key.

Client Anyone who has provided you with work.

Close (Deal) The final act in the process of selling a job. The close occurs with an agreement to exchange goods or services for compensation, usually accompanied by a contract and down payment.

Close (Spline curve) A command that joins the end vertices of a spline replace them with a single point.

Closed (Spline) A condition of a spline in MAX or AutoCAD (and other spline capable software) that is necessary before extrusion to create a complete solid.

Close-up A specific type of camera positioning that comes in on the subject to fill the screen with a singular or clearly defined image.

CMYK Cyan, magenta, yellow, and black ("b" is reserved for blue in RGB color systems) ink combinations used in printing systems.

Color bars A standard screen image used in the NTSC television standard. It consists of a screen of standard color rectangles used to calibrate broadcast equipment to an individual tape.

Color chips Samples of color provided by the client. These can be physical samples of a material or a sample that has a Pantone or other color system number associated with it.

Color depth Defined by the number of bits of the color byte used to describe each pixel of color in a file. The range is from one bit through sixty-four bit, with binary multiples in between.

Compression Small file sizes are always desirable and many technologies and formulas have been developed to make large files smaller. There are two types of compression: lossy and lossless.

Comps High quality printouts of a company's logo or product trademark.

Conditions of payment An agreement to exchange monies and goods conditional to certain conditions being met. An example would be payment in full upon delivery.

Contract An agreement negotiated between two parties for their mutual benefit.

Controller A subroutine of a program that carries out a specific function, such as turning two gears at a specific ratio for a specified period of time.

Copyrights Rights to your work that become yours upon completion of work; exclusions are work for hire or work sold under a complete buyout.

Cross fade A transition in which the end of one piece of film or animation fades away and is replaced by the fade-in of the next.

Cross reference A method of giving each document in a job information that connects it with another. An example is a job number that appears on each piece of paper created during the course of a job.

Cross section A view of what a part or assembly would look like if it were cut through along a specific plane or axis, it is intended to let you see what a thing would look like inside if you could cut it open.

Cursor The active point at which the mouse or other pointing device interacts with the monitor in a computer interface system.

Curvature The amount of bending across a distance on a line or surface. An arc is a simple curvature; more complex mathematics is needed to define irregular curves such as B-splines.

Cut A line along which a virtual object is split, or the point at which a scene in an animation terminates or is clipped.

D

Demo reel The calling card of an animator is his or her demo reel. It represents the best work they know how to produce and is their ticket to an interview for work.

Digital tape Most video recording is done on BETA or VHS tape. When higher quality such as film is to be the final result, the animation may be recorded on digital tape where the information can be stored in binary or digital format. With digital storage there is no loss or degradation when copies are made or editing is performed.

Dimaso An important variable to understand in order to assure accuracy when using AutoCAD. This variable determines whether the dimensions shown are actually interactive with the objects they define.

Dist An AutoCAD command that will feed back any distance between any two definable points on the screen and in the model.

Dope sheet A form developed for use with cell animation to define the location and duration of each image in an animation. It is an audio/visual timing device very adaptable to computer animation.

Dpi Dots/inch is the unit of measure of density of an image in printed material. 300 dpi is the density of most home printers today.

Dummy A nonrendering object used to connect other things such as a camera, light and spaceship for a journey through a tunnel.

E

Elevation view An architectural convention of looking at a structure straight on, such as a front view.

Engineering documents Text and drawings or graphical information associated with a job that will become a part of the history or paper trail of the work performed.

Establishing shot A camera angle chosen to give the viewer an overview or encompassing view of a broad area and define where a scene is taking place.

Expansion joint (concrete) The spaces created between segments of sidewalk and driveway. They serve to allow for expansion and contraction that occurs under different temperature and humidity conditions and to avoid random cracking.

Explode (AutoCAD) A command that breaks up larger groups or object blocks, meshes, or dimensions into smaller components. A dangerous use of this command separates an object from its dimensional control data.

Explode (MAX effect) Used to create the effect of an object breaking down into its component pieces (faces).

Extended primitives A package of new basic shapes that have been added to MAX.

Extents In AutoCAD, a predefined area in which to work. In MAX the area defined by the minima and maxima of the collective *x*, *y*, and *z* components of the elements of a model.

External annotation Notes or other information media that are intended to travel with a file or animation tape such as the label on a video tape (as opposed to internal annotation that is an integrated text add-on in a graphics file).

Extrude To extend a two-dimensional shape into the third dimension, usually to give it thickness.

F

F/x or special effects A variety of visual effects that include glow, sparkle, sparks, and morphing of shapes.

Face Three- or four-sided faces that define the smallest unit of divisibility of a virtual object. It is a surface definition that encompasses a renderable side, innate color, mapped materials, and special effects.

Fascia An architectural term used to describe the visible molding used between the roof and wall of a structure.

Fee plus A business agreement whereby work is performed for a flat fee plus other considerations, such as a percentage of a sale if a contract is secured using the animation.

Ferrule Usually a metal cap or cylinder used to brace a weak point in a wooden tool or structure or to form a transition between two unmatched diameters in an assembly.

Field of view The width and height of the image as seen through the camera lens.

File format The way a file is structured. Usually the beginning or end of a file contains documentation that the computer program uses to determine the rules about how to read the file and display its contents.

File/merge Taking information from one file and bringing it into an existing file. Libraries of models such as furniture are created as a resource for designers to use to "drop" furniture into a scene without redrawing it each time.

Filter A filter is used to select a group of components from a larger selection set, or as a device to interpret one format into another.

Fit/deform Using predefined curves to direct the shaping of a standard or more primitive form, such as using the profile curve of a staircase post to dynamically scale a circle as it lofts along a spline. May be performed along more than one axis at once.

Flares *See* camera flare.

Flat bed scanner A type of scanner where the image is placed on a flat sheet of glass and the scan head moves along the underside of the glass to take an impression. This type of scanner introduces very little distortion into the image.

Floppy An inexpensive storage medium that holds 1.44 megabytes of information.

Flying logo A term coined to mean a company logo advertising piece where the logo flies at the viewer and usually spins around.

Format *See* file format. Sometimes used to refer to standardized pieces of paper such as an architectural "D" which is 24" high by 36" inches wide, or the template from which standardized publication is created.

Fractal A mathematically generated, visually random graphic pattern. These patterns are often very organic in appearance and may some day form the basis of a highly effective compression system.

G

Gengon A generic primitive shape with various numbers of sides.

Glow A popular special effect that adds bright edges or an overall glow to the object(s) to which it is applied.

Gross The total amount of income you take in from a job or during a period or time before deducting expenses.

Ground plane The surface on which everything else resides. In architectural pieces, it is usually the earth; in engineering it may be a factory floor or a workbench (in small assembly).

Group A process of uniting elements that are not pieces of the same part but must act together, such as the body, wings, tail section and cockpit of a airplane. They are grouped so they stay together as the plane takes off.

H

Hard copy The printed version of an image.

Hard drive The primary data storage device in most personal computers.

Header (video) or heads The leader, blank, or still frames at the begining of an animation piece. It is a convenience to the editor rather than jumping from black into an animation.

Header (window) The horizontal piece across the top of a window.

Heads (video) or header *See* header.

Heat treatment A process applied to the teeth of gears to make them harder and more wear resistant.

Helix A spiral that winds into the *z* axis.

Hidden faces Faces can be visible or invisible, for various reasons; when a face is not seen, it is called a hidden face.

Highlight A spot or area where the light source is at right angles to a surface and reflecting straight at the viewer.

I

Incorporation A legal process that separates you from your business for reasons of liability, economics, or other reasons.

Instance A copy of an object that maintains a connection to the original in that some changes made to one occur in the copy automatically, as well.

Inverse kinematics A method of connecting otherwise unrelated parts together in a way that moving an extremity of the system affects the rest of the system.

Inverted face The normally visible side of some faces will sometimes be facing into an object rather than out, like it should. This occurs frequently with imported models where the originating package doesn't respect the same rules as the destination. These faces seem to vanish at rendering time and must be inverted.

J

JAZ A relatively inexpensive storage system with cartridges that hold one or two gigabytes of information.

K

Key frame A pivotal or transitional frame in an animation. Key frames are the change elements used by the computer to calculate the tweens, or inbetween frames.

Key way A slot cut into a mechanical part that takes a metal key to stop its rotation.

Kerning The process of respacing letters on a line of text to make them more pleasing visually.

Knurled Opposing grooves cut into a shaft to make it easier to grip.

L

LAYER (vector packages) A system that allows an artist to draw things on top of one another in stages that can be removed or shut off at will to make a specific detail easier to work on.

Layering A term usually applied to compositing video. Multiple images are placed on top of one another. Transparency of some of the layers, naturally occurring or digitally forced, that allows the viewer to see many overlapping images.

Lead (sales) In sales, it is necessary to make an initial connection within your target market before making an appointment. Finding a lead is the first step toward making a sale.

Lead (camera) To lead is a term applied to camera action in which the camera looks in a direction before the actor changes direction and moves in that direction.

Lens flare *See* flare.

Letter of intent Often takes the place of a more complex contract. The document states the intention of both parties and is legally binding in court.

Letterhead Usually a printed form, on 8 1/2" x 11" bond paper, showing the logo (if any), name, address, contact information and phone number of a company.

Liability The extent to which you become legally responsible for the results of your work. Legal animation is one area where you can become legally entangled because of your work.

Loft A process whereby you define a shape as it is created in the third dimension by controlling the cross sections along that length.

Loft path The path along which a loft takes place.

Logo A company's symbol or trademark.

M

Machine shop Usually a small business that subcontracts to larger firms consisting of several pieces of manufacturing equipment such as an end mill, lathe, table saw, and surface grinder.

Manufacturing company Any business that delivers a mechanical retail product to the market.

Map Two-dimensional images that can be placed or painted onto a three-dimensional object, such as brick on a wall.

Mapping icon A nonprinting or rendering symbol that shows the direction and orientation at which a map will be placed on an object. It is manipulated separately from the object itself.

Mask An image that defines what part of another image is not shown or becomes transparent, usually black and white or grayscale.

Masthead *See* letterhead.

Material ID A numbering system that allows different parts of the same object to have different materials, e.g., a head can have flesh tones on the face and hair texture on the hair region.

Materials editor A window in which materials are created.

Materials scaling A method of creating a properly scaled relatioship, usually one-to-one, between the size of a map and the object it is placed on.

Meg Common abbreviation for one megabyte of computer data equal to one million binary bits.

Mil. Abbreviation used in the plastics and coating industries to indicate a thickness of .001, or one thousandth part of an inch.

Milestone points Indication or check points along a timeline between receipt of a job and the completion date.

Millwork Wood that has been processed, usually by power shaping one or more surfaces such as the decorative molding between the ceiling and walls in a home.

Mirror image Being handed, having an otherwise identical but opposite facing pairing of an object.

Modify pivot A selection sequence that allows operator selection of the default or previous pivot point of an object. Used to control rotation.

Monochrome Usually used to mean shades of gray or the value-only representation of an image. Can also be used to mean a picture based primarily or entirely on one hue as in monochromatic.

Motion lines Cartoon, storyboard, and comic book icons for indicating motion. Usually represented as trailing lines indicating where corners have been in space.

Mullion A vertical dividing bar between windows or lites of glass.

N

Net Business term meaning the gross income from a job or period of time less all expenses. Can mean the profit.

NTSC National Television Standards Committee. Defines size, signal, ratios, colors, and other broadcast standards for the televison industry.

Nurbs Non-uniform rational b-splines. A system for modeling that defines surfaces with curves rather than polygons.

O

Operational prototype Ergonomic and sales mockups of a potential product may define shape, feel, color, and texture only; an operational model is a fully functioning version of a device.

Organic shape All models can be defined as geometric or organic, or a combination of the two; organic models have smooth, flowing lines rather than angular relationships.

Osnap An AutoCAD command that gives access to how the cursor seeks and finds geometric points on a line or model, such as the endpoint of a line or center of an arc.

Output Generic term meaning any format in which the computer gives the operator the results of work. May be a view of data on the screen or a hard copy print or plot on paper.

Overhead The costs of doing business: travel expenses, paper goods, printer supplies, and the cost of the computer itself are all overhead.

Overhead (file size) All modeling decisions affect the size of the file that is being created. Since large files are slower for the computer to handle and render, file size becomes a kind of overhead or cost to the model builder.

P

Pan A method of sliding the operator's view across the screen without changing the scale, or side-sliding the camera in a scene.

Pantone A precise matching system that defines color in terms of its CMYK or print ink equivalent. The system uses color swatches and numbers to specify percentages of the four ink colors and spot colors that are named.

Patch A two-dimensional area that can be manipulated or modeled in three-dimensional space to form a desired shape.

Penalty A fine that is agreed upon between parties in a contract for failure to comply with a condition of that contract.

Perimeter An unbroken line around the walls or foundation of a building that can be extruded to form the basic shape of a model.

Perspective matching Giving information to the computer, extracted from a background image (still or animation) and using the horizon gained from that process to overlay a model on the background, at the same perspective angle.

Perspective view A view based on vanishing points and foreshortening with respect to distance from the viewer.

Pitch (architectural) The angle of a roof measured as a ratio off the horizontal as the rise, or *y*-value, divided by or over the run or corresponding *x*-value.

Pitch (printing) In printing, defines intercharacter spacing in a line.

Pitch (sales) Any presentation or talk to a buying party intended to sway them to make a purchase or commit to a contract.

Plan view Architectural term meaning the view of a project seen straight down or bird's eye, usually drawn to show internal elements as well, without the roof in place.

Plug-in manager A program that manages other programs, loads utilities or special effects routines on demand.

Points A printer's system for measuring text height; there are 72 points to each inch.

Polygon Multisided shape, usually regular.

Polyline A B-spline curve available in AutoCAD with many controllable and desirable characteristics.

Preview A rendering mode in MAX that creates a simplified .AVI file version of an animation showing only value and one color for review purposes.

Primitive A basic shape; usually the base for further refinement of an object.

Primitive, extended One of a group of recently expanded set of primitives.

Procedural materials A material whose overall look and texture is based on a mathematical description rather than a picture: wood, marble, water, and sand are good candidates for this type of surface treatment.

Proof Usually an inexpensive, low-resolution version of the final product, used for approval purposes.

Proposal An outline or description of work that can be done. Usually prepared at the request of a client by a contractor.

Proprietary Created for a specific client, not for resale or distribution. May be machinery, a methodology, or software meant to perform a task specific to that company.

Props Objects added to the staging of a scene to enhance the message or story.

Prototype Usually a one-of-a-kind item created to test the possibility of manufacturing that item in larger quantities.

Purchase order (P.O.) A numbered document issued by a company or corporation; a request for work to be done. Usually states the price to be paid and any company policies.

Purchasing agent An individual in a large company who has the authority to buy for the company. This person is often the one who gives the final approval to proceed with work.

Q

Quote A document and a step in the sales process after the bid and before the contract; acceptance of the quote, in writing, is often used in lieu of a contract or letter of intent.

R

Radius The distance from the center of an arc or circle to a point on the circle.

Raster *See* Appendix A, raster vs. vector.

Reference material Any material used for information purposes, loosely interpreted or tightly traced or copied. Ownership of such material is the primary copyright issue.

Regenerate or update A step in the creation process in many graphics packages whereby the operator instructs the program to reread the file to correct or refresh the display.

Release A document with which rights are defined or relinquished. You get a release from a model for the rights to use and display their image.

Remedies Contractual solutions to breaches of the contract, such as paying a penalty per day for failure to deliver the job on time.

Rendering Instructing the computer to calculate the resultant image based on the parameters set in the software. The final process whereby the computer calculates each frame of the animation.

Rendering time The time it will take to render the individual frames or the entire series required for the complete animation.

Revision Changes made to the product after the original information has been released. May be as simple as adding a different color material to a chair or a radical change in the structure. All revisions should be accompanied by a document; a fax is sufficient and a fee for any changes should be a clause in the contract.

Revsurf An AutoCAD function that gives the operator exceptional control of face generation on the model. Allows a degree of accuracy not available using the AutoCAD function REVOLVE or the MAX LATHE command.

RGB Red, green and blue are the colors used to specify images defined with light. The VGA monitor of your computer and your TV use a RGB color system.

Rotoscoping An animation process used to trace or directly capture motion from video or film to animation cells. The term is also used to describe the process of applying an animated material to a virtual object.

Ruler tool A tool in MAX that allows indirect measurement of objects, acts as a ruler of prespecified length or can measure existing objects.

S

Sales promotion Any activity that helps make your market aware of your presence and capabilities.

Sans serif Type is grouped into two general categories; serif (a design with flourishes or tails)and sans serif (plain in design).

Scale time The process of adding frames to an animation effectively making the whole piece longer and stretching the action out at the same time (as opposed to simply adding blank frames on the end or beginning).

Scale uniform An object is made larger or smaller by an equal proportion along all three axes at the same time.

Scanning Capturing an image into the computer in an electronic, usually raster, format.

Segments The number of pieces or polygons used to make a curved surface look smooth or rounded. The greater the number of segments used, the smoother the object will look and the larger the file that is created.

Select rotate The select rotate tool can select and then rotate in a single operation; the commands are combined.

Self-promotion Any activity that helps make your market aware of your presence and capabilities. Also applies to a right you have in your work even after it is sold, to use that work to promote yourself.

Serif A tail or flourish added to some typefaces.

Service bureau A graphics contracting business that accepts (among other things) electronic graphics and produces high quality output or bulk printing. Most have binding and delivery services also.

Set screw A headless screw used to lock a mechanical device in place on a shaft such as a gear or pulley.

Sill Architectural term meaning the horizontal trim at the bottom of a window. May also have an additional apron below the sill.

SMPTE A precise time code used to coordinate editing and camera changes in the film industry. It consists of hours, minutes, seconds and hundredths of seconds.

Smear An undesirable effect caused by improper mapping of the edges of a model.

Smooth (material) Create matching smoothing group values between faces to cause the calculation of those surfaces as curved at rendering.

Smooth (mechanical) An automated process that adds additional faces to a model to make it appear smoother.

Spec., or speculative work Work that is paid for only if it is chosen or selected by the client. It is discouraged and considered to be an unacceptable practice by professional illustrators.

Special effects, or f/x Any visual device that that does not fall into the basic animation categories of modeling, material editing, lighting, model or camera movement or output to media. Includes explosions, rotoscoped materials, volume lights, fog, flare, and many other effects.

Spline A curve that is defined by passing through or being influenced by the presence of fixed points in space.

Spokes Legs that radiate from a hub and connect the hub to the outer portion of a wheel, usually radial.

Stack An interactive list of the operations that have been performed on a primitive.

Stacking segments An undesirable condition whereby smaller line segments are coincident with longer segments and cause errors in dimensioning, dividing, and arraying objects.

Still images A picture or single frame from an animation.

Stock photos Pictures that are sold from catalogues to use as reference or as an element in other, finished work.

Stock metal Uncut, unprocessed, or semi-finished metal.

Story The basis of animation. The animator is a visual or graphic storyteller.

Storyboard A display or presentation piece consisting of simplified images depicting key frames. Helps to clarify the animation before more time-consuming and expensive commitments are made.

Stucco A rough-textured, cement-based material used on walls.

Subcontract Work performed for a negotiated fee (not for a salary or wage).

Subdirectory A device used in conjunction with computer hard drives to organize files; structure based on files and folders.

Surftab 1 & 2 The variables that control the REVSURF command.

Symmetrical The same, but mirrored on either side of an axis.

T

Tail(s) or trailer An extension of black frames or copies of the last frame repeated for 30 or more frames as a courtesy to the editor.

Taper A modifier that makes one end of a primitive smaller or larger than the other.

Teeth (gear) The part of a gear or pair of gears that actually engage or mesh with one another.

Timeline A visual representation of the future history of a job, usually starts when the contract is signed and ends at the delivery date. Milestones along the path are created to test the progress of the job.

Toggle A switch with on and off, or sometimes three distinct positions. A binary switch as opposed to an analog or adjustable slider.

Torus The geometry name for a doughnut.

Trailer or tails *See* tails.

Transition A video post-processing effect that defines a movement from the end of one animation or video segment to the beginning of another. The simplest transition is a cut.

Tube A cylinder that is hollow end to end.

U

Unstable model Depending on their method of creation, some models, after Boolean operations have been performed, will act erratically at rendering time. Some simply vanish. Others will shoot vertices off into space or otherwise deform, or crash the program.

User view This is an isometric view of the model, as opposed to a perspective view (that uses vanishing points) or a camera view (that uses a lens perspective view).

V

Vector A line that has a definite start point but travels infinitely in one direction (AutoCAD useage). Description-based file, as opposed to a raster file, which is pixel based.

Vent A slotted opening in the peak or roof of a building intended to let hot air escape from the attic.

Vertex A single point, it may define the intersection of the corners of faces in a polymesh. It can be a stand-alone point or define the intersection of many faces.

VHS Standard tape for recording NTSC video.

VHS Gold High quality VHS tape.

Video card The printed circuit board and associated hardware that controls the image on your computer monitor.

Video post-processing Any image that is added over or in addition to images produced with the standard program or camera.

Video recorder A device that writes video information to video tape.

Video tape Magnetic media (magnetic iron oxide compounds bonded to mylar plastic)to which binary or analog information can be written.

Virtual model A model of something that can be manipulated within the computer but doesn't exist in the physical reality.

Voice-over Voice of an unseen narrator in a video.

W

Weld (vertex) A process of joining points in a model or between patches to make them shared between two or more faces.

Welded (metals) A process of melting two pieces of metal and adding additional metal at the same point to create a single piece.

Z

ZIP drive A relatively inexpensive storage device and cartridge arrangement. Each cartridge holds approximately 100 megabytes, about as much as 80 floppy disks.

Index